For Jessie and Patrick

and

For Abby, David, and Yukari,

With hope politics will improve in the next generation

Jack W. Germond

FAT MAN
Fed Up

★ ★ ★ HOW AMERICAN POLITICS WENT BAD ★ ★ ★

RANDOM HOUSE / NEW YORK

LIBRARY OF CONGRESS CATALOGING-IN-PUBLICATION DATA
Germond, Jack.
Fat man fed up: how American politics went bad / Jack W. Germond.
p. cm.
Includes index.
ISBN 1-4000-6154-7
1. United States—Politics and government—1945–1989.   2. United States—Politics
and government—1989–   3. Politicians—United States—Anecdotes.   4. Press and
politics—United States.   5. Presidents—United States—Election.   6. Elections—United
States.   7. Political campaigns—United States.   8. Political culture—United States.
9. Germond, Jack W.   10. Journalists—United States—Biography.   I. Title.
E839.5.G394 2004
070'.92—dc22   2004041856

Printed in the United States of America on acid-free paper

Random House website address: www.atrandom.com

246897531

FIRST EDITION

Book design by Casey Hampton

In America anybody can become president.
That's just one of the risks you take.

—ADLAI E. STEVENSON

FAT MAN FED UP

ACKNOWLEDGMENTS AND CAVEATS

This book is a product of my fifty years as a newspaper reporter, which I enjoyed immensely. It is a career I have given up only because, with age, I have lost the edge off my fastball and I don't want to be forced to rely on slow curves and other forms of guile to cover the story. I still relish the company of the reporters, politicians, and campaign operatives whom I count as my friends. Given those premises, this book may seem counterintuitive, to the degree that it is a harsh critique of the press as well as of the voters and the politicians. All three have contributed heavily to what I consider a disheartening decline in American politics.

I am not viewing this decline from the mountaintop, however. As a newspaper reporter and columnist, I have contributed to this cheapening of the process. On more occasions than I like to remember, I have written dumb stories about issues created out of the mists that no intelligent reader should have been asked to take seriously. As a television commentator, I have too often held forth on camera about issues about which I knew only enough to hum a few bars. Mea culpa.

I am indebted to my editor at Random House, Jonathan Jao, who has shown a good eye for lapses in logic and other miscellaneous offenses I have committed, and to my agent, David Black, who encouraged me to vent on paper as I have done.

My wife, Alice, has once again been of incalculable help with her ear for false notes and inconsistencies. She has helped me shape this book in countless ways while, in a most loving way, keeping my ego under control.

These days I find it necessary to stress that the stories I relate here are all stories I covered myself as a reporter. I have plagiarized only myself by repeating a few anecdotes from my own memoir and the four books on presidential campaigns I wrote with Jules Witcover, my friend and longtime partner in our column at the *Washington Star* and the Baltimore *Sun*.

In the interest of full disclosure, I should add that Alice Germond is the secretary of the Democratic National Committee and a veteran of several Democratic presidential campaigns. However, my biases are my own.

Jack W. Germond
Charles Town, West Virginia
February 2004

CONTENTS

FAT MAN FED UP

IN DEFENSE OF POLITICIANS

*W*hen I was a young reporter covering city hall for the *Evening News* in Monroe, Michigan, the publisher suggested one day that I should write an occasional editorial on local issues. Fired with the self-righteous certitude of youth, I leaped at the chance. I would straighten out those hacks on the city commission whose meetings I was obliged to cover every Monday night.

But the publisher, a wise man named JS Gray, cautioned me to be patient. "Don't nip at their heels," he said. "We get about what we deserve"—meaning that the quality of the city government reflected the seriousness with which the voters of Monroe considered their decisions when choosing commissioners. We had the proprietor of a small dry-goods store, a salesman in a haberdashery, the operator of a service station, and a couple of young lawyers on the hustle. They were all nice enough people, but we didn't have the municipal equivalent of Robert Taft or Sam Rayburn. So, by JS Gray's reckoning, we shouldn't expect too much.

He was right. Today, after fifty years of exposure to thousands of politicians, I am convinced that we get about what we deserve at all levels of government, up to and including the White House. These days, because so many Americans—almost half—don't bother to vote even in presidential elections, they deserve choices like the one they were offered in 2000, between Al Gore and George W. Bush. Because so few Americans understand the political process or bother to follow it with even a modicum of attention, we elect presidents as empty as George H. W. Bush or as self-absorbed as Bill Clinton—only to be followed by a choice between a Republican obviously over his head and a Democrat too unsure of his own persona to be convincing.

As a group, it turns out, politicians are just like everyone else in our society—a few men and women of high quality, many of different levels of mediocrity, and, finally, a few knaves and poltroons. There are members of Congress who would be overpaid at ten thousand dollars a year and others who would be underpaid at a half million. Nor are presidents of the United States men of some extra dimension, a phrase favored by Richard M. Nixon, other than perhaps the tenacious ambition required to win the office. On the contrary, our presidents are, perhaps too often, very ordinary people.

It is also clear, however, that politicians, whatever their failings, are better people than they are depicted to be in much of the news media and reputed to be in the popular wisdom.

They are men and women who have the nerve to put themselves out there for a popular verdict on their performance and potential delivered in the most public way. Spend an election night with a candidate and you cannot help but be impressed by how wrenching the process can be even for one who is winning. Sure, I'm getting 60 percent of the vote, the candidate mutters to himself, but what about that other 40 percent? Where did I go wrong with them? What can I do to get them next time? They always hope to pitch a shutout.

Many politicians can be good company. They have topics beyond the price of real estate on which they are knowledgeable and interesting. Moreover, they usually have objective minds despite the partisan nature of their work. Often they show, offstage at least, a wicked sense of humor. But they are frequently the victims of grossly inaccurate perceptions.

Contrary to widespread suspicions, for example, they are not in politics for the money. There are exceptions, of course—a few politicians so grasping and perhaps arrogant that they cannot resist the "good things" put in their way by those who want something. They leap at the hot stocks or real estate deals or commodities futures that suddenly appear once they attain power and a position to reward their friends. But most of those who succeed in politics even to the modest level of a seat in the House of Representatives could make a lot more money elsewhere.

Politicians are not hard to read. Their goal is influence rather than money. Wherever they are, they want to take the next step up the ladder. While shaving, the city councilman muses about a seat in the state legislature, where his thoughts quickly turn to Congress, and who knows where that might lead? Ask a candidate for president where he got the idea to run in the first place, and he will usually confess that it came from observing the other candidates and the guy who's already in office.

When I visited Governor Jimmy Carter of Georgia for a catfish dinner in Atlanta in 1974, I asked him where he ever got the idea he could be president. "From getting to know the rest of them," he replied, "when they come here to visit." When I encountered one of "the rest of them," Senator Lloyd Bentsen of Texas, a few months later and asked him the same question, his reply was almost identical.

I also remember calling on Senator Ernest Hollings in 1983 after hearing he was quietly raising some political money back home in South Carolina. When I confronted him with my suspicion that he was "thinking about running for president," he replied in that rich South Carolina drawl, "Jack, all senators think about it all the time."

We'll never know how many young politicians there are like Bill Clinton, who had his eye already fixed on the White House when I met him as a thirty-year-old state attorney general running for governor of Arkansas in 1978. But they are not hard to find. For years I made reporting stops in several states a year to meet a local hot property someone had told me enjoyed great potential in national politics—a lieutenant governor such as Mark Hogan of Colorado or Ben

Barnes of Texas or perhaps a mayor such as Kevin White of Boston or Jerry Cavanagh of Detroit. Just as every small town has a pitcher who can throw his fastball through a wall, every state has a political phenom who seems destined for the majors. The question is always whether he can throw a curveball, too.

The critical point, however, is that politicians usually want the higher office and the influence it offers in order to achieve some purpose beyond money or their own self-aggrandizement. They have goals that voters may or may not applaud but that are nonetheless legitimate ends they might achieve by gaining a voice in public policy. And we should find some comfort in the transparency of their motives, even if we don't agree with, for example, their determination to turn the national parks over to the oil companies.

So why do we think so poorly of them? Why do so many Americans consider the business too "dirty" to claim their attention? And certainly too dirty to participate in themselves. These days, for most Americans the notion of attending a Republican or Democratic meeting in their ward is laughable. Running for precinct chairman is ludicrous. What is a ward anyway? What's a precinct? The days when ward leaders passed out turkeys at Thanksgiving are long gone.

One reason for this popular disdain is, of course, the few politicians who behave so badly they deserve the contempt with which they are regarded. These are the ones who use their positions to enrich themselves and their friends. The ones who will do anything to be elected and once elected will roll over for any lobbyist or special interest. The ones whose performance in office is such an egregious embarrassment that some people actually notice.

A second factor is the rhetoric of so many politicians who make a career out of denigrating their own calling and presenting themselves as the exception who will clean up the whole ugly mess. When Americans spend eight years listening to Ronald Reagan disparage politicians—he loved to carry on about "draining the swamp" in Washington—it should be no surprise that potential voters turn away. Who wants to be a party to something so rotten?

Others in high places devalue the political life by the example they set. What would thoughtful Americans believe to be the lesson, for example, from the two most important appointments President George Herbert Walker Bush ever made?

The first was the choice—twice—of Dan Quayle for vice president. What did that tell us about the value the elder Bush attached to the highest office in the land? The second was his selection of Clarence Thomas for the Supreme Court. What was that all about other than using the appointment of an African American as a way of saying nyah-nyah to the Democrats? What did it tell voters about the importance of the nation's highest court? That it was just another political asset? If we have to live with it for another thirty years, too bad.

Conventional wisdom also holds that we think so badly of politicians because the news media, broadly defined, cedes so much of its voice to a few columnists and the braying jackasses of talk radio and cable television. But anyone with a long memory in politics knows that the conspiracy theorists and dark dissenters have always been with us, suggesting that the Rush Limbaughs of this age have mined an existing population of yahoos rather than creating one from scratch.

This is a bloc—yahoos in my perhaps jaundiced view—substantial enough to be heard but still a minority of Americans. Assailing a proposed pay raise for Congress, for example, Limbaugh has shown he can flood the mailbags and telephone lines of Capitol Hill with angry protests at a time when opinion polls of the electorate at large show voters about evenly divided on the same issue. It is even possible to uncover a plurality of Americans tolerant of an increase when they hear the arguments justifying it. That dichotomy suggests that the Limbaugh audience is not an accurate sample of the electorate as a whole, which should come as no surprise.

When I once suggested this in a television broadcast, Limbaugh accused me of saying that his listeners were not entitled to be heard. His braying set off a barrage of telephone calls to me in Washington and to the editors of my newspaper, the Baltimore *Sun,* demanding that I be fired, at the least, or better yet, immolated. It was the most emotional reaction I have ever evoked with anything I wrote or said on television.

This assault on my bona fides as a human being went on for a week or two until by chance I showed up at the annual Radio-TV Correspondents Association dinner at a time when Limbaugh was testing a pilot for a television program. A camera crew from that program approached me during the cocktail hour for an interview. I was abashed at the notion but felt I couldn't refuse. As it turned out, it gave me a golden opportunity. When the interviewer asked what I thought of Rush Limbaugh going on television, I replied that I thought it was great because "we need more fat guys on television." As I recall it, I mentioned "fat guys" several times. End of problem.

Whatever their limits, Limbaugh and his imitators have provided some cohesion and coherence to the minority of Americans who like to rant about the folly of liberalism. And the liberals have helped them along by being so stuffy and self-righteous and so easy to skewer. Taken in very small doses, Rush Limbaugh can be funny. Not so John Kenneth Galbraith.

The distrust of politicians is not fostered by the Limbaughs alone, however. It is part of the operating ethic of the mainstream news media to keep a close watch on public officials and the taxpayers' money. And it is a legitimate function when performed responsibly. But too often both newspapers and television-news organizations project a picture of themselves wringing their hands in glee at exposing these crooks in public life.

The broadcast-television networks, today's single most important provider of news, love stories about how "it's your money" (ABC News) that is being wasted in "the fleecing of America" (NBC News). Newspapers win Pulitzer Prizes for exposés of official misconduct. Reporters love to tell one another old war stories about how they exposed some mayor paving his driveway with public asphalt or some sewer commissioner with his hands in the till. But reporters rarely boast of the stories they wrote about honest politicians doing what they were elected to do. In fact, only the best newspapers bother to provide any detail on the workings of government that might lead a few readers to be less hostile to all elected officials.

Local television can be particularly brutal because its political coverage is so unsophisticated—too often little more than some twinkie, male or female, repeating slogans learned from their betters. They do not hesitate to make broad judgments that go well beyond the diligence and skill of their reporting. A typical case involved a state senator from Florida who had spent years in Tallahassee building knowledge and expertise and earning widespread respect from his peers in both parties. There are people like him in every state legislature, as well as in Congress—politicians who are also public officials who take their jobs seriously and devote far more time to them than is required. One year, however, this senator made the mistake of attending the annual meeting of the National Conference of State Legislatures held in that capital of sin, New Orleans. Although he met his responsibilities by attending the conference and going to the business sessions, he made the fatal blunder of driving over to Biloxi at night to gamble in the casinos that line the stretch of the Gulf Coast known as the Redneck Riviera.

What he didn't expect was a camera crew from a hometown TV station that followed him and reported on his high living in glamorous Biloxi when presumably he should have been spending his leisure discussing land-use planning with fellow legislators from Montana. In fact, since no taxpayer money was involved in the side trip to Biloxi, there wasn't a legitimate story there. But the TV crew made it sound like another case of a politician shirking his duties for his own pleasure and profit.

Given everything voters hear and read, their harsh view of public officials is inevitable. Most Americans, unhappily, are too lazy or uninterested to question whether press accounts of malfeasance present a balanced view. When the sainted Ralph Nader revives the mantra of the late George Corley Wallace and insists that there is not a dime's worth of difference between the two major political parties, it sounds sort of sensible. Many voters like the idea of being "independents" who vote "for the man, not the party."

Enough Americans accepted that notion of civic virtue to alter the outcome of the 2000 presidential election, when votes for Nader clearly defeated Al Gore and elected George W. Bush. (The same thing probably happened in 1968, when George Wallace took enough votes from Hubert H. Humphrey to elect Richard M. Nixon.)

Nader's insistence that there was no difference in the parties was hard to swallow after Bush made John Ashcroft the attorney general and gained control of the makeup of the Supreme Court. But the self-less Nader was catnip for voters who think politics is a little dirty but still wanted to perform their civic duty by casting their ballots. It seemed to make them feel warm and virtuous. They should be ashamed of their naïveté and embarrassed at the price Americans were forced to pay as a result. Ralph Nader has done many worthwhile things for this country; running for president has not been one of them.

The most obvious product of the contempt for politics and politicians is, however, the decline in voting rather than the decline in the quality of the candidates. In the 1996 presidential election some sort of nadir was reached. Voter turnout, 49.1 percent of the voting-age population, reached its lowest level since 1924. Considering the growth in literacy and the corresponding growth in sources of "information" since 1924, that was a message of alarm in neon letters ten feet tall.

The downward spiral has been evident for over a generation. The turnout was 63 percent in 1960, 62 percent in 1964, and 61 percent in 1968. But it dropped to 55 percent to reelect Richard Nixon in 1972, 54 percent in the "Watergate election" of 1976, and 53 percent in both the 1980 and 1984 victories of Reagan. Ever since then it has been around 50 percent, except in 1992, when the Ross Perot candidacy increased the universe of voters to 55 percent of those who were eligible.

Apparently most Americans don't care who is president these days. And the campaigns the politicians run don't seem able to crack that wall of indifference.

You might expect the campaigns that dominate the television screens for months every four years would engage the interest of more potential voters. But the truth is that the political dialogue in this country today has little or nothing to do with the lives of most Americans. They know it, but the press doesn't seem to understand it—and neither do many of the politicians or the consultants who tell them what to do.

And that, of course, is the reason campaigns are such useless exercises.

2

THE MINDLESS CAMPAIGN

*I*n theory a political campaign is supposed to be, at least in part, an educational experience for the voters. The idea is that they will learn not only about the candidates' histories and positions on the issues of the day but also something about their personal qualities. Then, the theory goes, they will be able to make their choices with some confidence. And that confidence, in turn, should encourage them to vote.

Fat chance. It happens once in a while, perhaps by accident. But even presidential election campaigns, with all their concentration of media attention for so many months, rarely tell voters what they need to know to make an informed decision. Did Americans get any idea in 2000, for example, that Iraq was such a bone in the throat of George W. Bush? Essentially all they were told about his foreign policy was that he intended to make Colin Powell secretary of State. And as we discovered, that didn't tell you much, considering how little influence Powell enjoyed.

At the lower levels of politics, informative campaigns are rare enough that they become legend and people in the political community talk about them long afterward. In Massachusetts, the home field for many vivid political battles, the most memorable of recent generations was the 1996 Senate contest in which the incumbent Democrat, John F. Kerry, was challenged by an engaging Republican governor, William Weld. They confronted each other in seven debates that gave voters a far better picture than they usually see of Senate candidates. Even the most jaded Boston pols bragged about it for years.

But this was an exception. Most campaigns are not designed to give voters an accurate picture of the choices they face. In fact, they are often designed to achieve the opposite result. All the money is spent by the campaign strategists—usually the paid consultants—to present their candidates in the most favorable light and their opponents in the darkest shadows. We shouldn't be surprised about this. Even the sainted Adlai Stevenson recognized (although he did not act on the premise) that "the first duty of any politician is to get elected."

How things got this way is no mystery. The huge amounts of money flowing into politics in the television age have created a world in which political consultants have multiplied in geometric proportions. It seems that no campaign can be without them. Indeed, one of the credentials used by the press and politicians to classify a campaign as "serious" is the roster of consultants the candidate has signed for twenty or thirty thousand dollars a month plus a cut of the television buy. If someone has hired James Carville, the theory goes, he must be a serious candidate.

And once all these experts with all that money to spend offer their advice, the candidates seem obliged to go along with it. There are candidates who resist and even refuse the gimmicks recommended to them by the consultants, but they are the exceptions rather than the rule. The result, unsurprisingly, is most often a contrived, mechanistic campaign that tells us nothing about a candidate beyond his ability to understand and act on opinion-poll results.

Despite Stevenson, the liberal Democrats are most often the ones who rely on the wisdom and good intentions of "the people" to prevail in the end. In June 1988 I asked Michael S. Dukakis, the Democratic candidate for president, how he was going to deal with the

Republican use of the American flag issue. It had arisen when the Massachusetts governor, acting on the advice of his state attorney general, refused to order a daily recital of the Pledge of Allegiance in public school classrooms because, he said, it would violate the separation of church and state. Now the Republicans were depicting this as evidence of a lack of patriotism on the part of Dukakis, who was the son of immigrants and a veteran of the Korean War.

But Dukakis shrugged it off. The voters, he told me, were too smart to fall for something that ridiculous. He was wrong. It was ridiculous indeed, but they weren't smart enough to see it. After George H. W. Bush, who boasted that he would do anything to get elected, visited a flag factory in New Jersey during the campaign, the Dukakis strategists realized they had a "flag problem" on their hands. But it was too late. The issue haunted Dukakis throughout the campaign.

Four years earlier another liberal Democratic nominee for president, Walter F. Mondale, had shown a similar childlike faith in the electorate when he closed his acceptance speech at the nominating convention in San Francisco by telling Americans that both he and the incumbent president, Ronald Reagan, would be forced to raise taxes in the years ahead but that he was the only one willing to face the facts. It was true, of course, but the truth is often the first casualty in American campaigns. So all Mondale earned was the derision of the political community, including many of his Democratic supporters, for daring to speak the truth on taxes and trust "the people." That almost always qualifies as a gaffe.

The length to which campaigns will go demonstrates the contempt in which many of those who run them—particularly the consultants— hold both voters and the press. They do outlandish things without fearing a penalty because they know, first, that the voters are not paying enough attention to be offended, and second, that the mainstream press doesn't give them any reason to be. No one in the press says bluntly to the electorate: If you fall for this, you're a sucker. Many of the better newspapers have assigned good reporters to analyze campaign commercials in search of misstatements and lies. But such feeble attempts at truth telling pale when compared with vivid television spots.

The 1988 Bush campaign provided another example of how far a candidate will go, one that I consider the most indefensible in my fifty years of covering politics at every level, from that city commission in Monroe, Michigan, to the White House. In October George H. W. Bush held a rally at Christ the King High School in Queens. The audience was made up largely of several hundred well-scrubbed kids waving small American flags provided by the campaign and cheering for the death penalty, a warming spectacle. The purpose, ostensibly, was for Bush to accept the endorsement of his candidacy by the Police Benevolent Association, and the stage was packed with impressive ranks of uniformed cops.

In fact, the PBA endorsement had been voted, delivered, and reported a week or so earlier, but this was an excuse for another round of stories and another television-news clip of the candidate surrounded by masses of cops. It made a hell of a picture. Who would remember this was an old story? Who would care?

There was, moreover, one new element to the story. A police officer named Ed Byrne had been killed while trying to make a drug arrest a few days earlier, and his grieving father, Matthew, was on the stage. He announced he was forming a foundation in his son's name and—to the point here—was presenting his martyred son's police shield to Vice President Bush.

The Republican candidate accepted the badge in a moment taut with emotion throughout the auditorium, then blithely turned the occasion into political trash by saying: "If the liberal governor of Massachusetts doesn't understand it when a Matt Byrne stands up and creates a foundation for his son, I do, and so do the American people."

It was a moment of breathtakingly crass behavior from this product of privilege, Andover, and Yale. But it passed almost unremarked in the mindless politics and political journalism of our time. One local-television report that night focused on the kids cheering while Bush demanded the electric chair. The Republican candidate's monstrous suggestion that Dukakis would not share his sympathy with Matt

Byrne never made a ripple. These days a candidate must accuse his rival of bestiality or necrophilia before anyone raises an eyebrow.

Bizarre accusations are not limited to presidential politics, of course. If anything, voters pay even less attention at the lower levels and are thus vulnerable to even more outlandish attacks. In 2000, in a particularly egregious case, a deservedly obscure Republican congressman named Saxby Chambliss unseated Senator Max Cleland of Georgia by depicting him as lacking the patriotic fervor to support President Bush's war on terrorism because he voted against the White House homeland security bill. In fact, like most Democrats, Cleland voted for an alternative that would have accomplished the same purpose in a somewhat different way to protect the union position of federal workers.

The most offensive thing was the Chambliss commercials attacking Cleland that pictured him along with Osama bin Laden and Saddam Hussein—thus questioning the loyalty of a man who had lost both legs and an arm on the battlefield during the Vietnam War, in which Chambliss did not serve. It was mind-boggling, but it worked. There is no penalty for bad behavior in American politics. No one is paying attention.

There appears to be a generational divide on issues like this. When I recounted Bush's incredible statement about Dukakis to my contemporaries covering the campaign, they were as repulsed as I had been. But the political reporters of the next generation shrugged it off. They had become accustomed to such garbage, perhaps because they had seen so little else. And the voters, of course, write off the most venal politics as something to be expected. The theory is that they all do it, which is wrong but accepted.

Indeed, there are occasional and encouraging signs that a few voters may be paying attention to the tone of the campaigns. In the Democratic presidential primaries of 2004, for example, Senator John Edwards of North Carolina made himself the last man standing against Senator John Kerry largely by running a conspicuously positive campaign. The response from Democrats voting in those contests suggested an appreciation of Edwards's approach and, in some cases, a reaction against the usual negative attack politics. But such cases are the rare exceptions and perhaps more likely in primary situations, where those who even bother to vote are probably paying closer attention to the campaign.

Given the distance kept by the electorate in most elections, the most successful strategists in presidential campaigns are those who rely on a mechanistic approach that is as unrevealing as possible. The goal every day is to score a favorable "hit" on the network-television news broadcasts—meaning a good picture and a brief repetition of the message of the day—while keeping the candidate insulated from the real world and the press.

When this approach is carried to the extreme, we are treated to campaigns like the one in 2000 between Al Gore and George W. Bush, in which voters were never given any real insight into either candidate. Didn't George Bush have to be smarter than he seemed? Was Al Gore really such a stiff? How could you tell? Most candidates seem to do what they are told.

Gore provided an example in the fall 1999 preliminaries to the New Hampshire primary. By chance, on the September day local newspapers reported a poll showing that Gore had fallen behind his rival for the nomination, Senator Bill Bradley, the candidate turned up at an afternoon campaign gathering at a park in Keene. When the local reporters accosted him, Gore told them he actually liked being behind at this stage of the campaign, apparently on the theory that it would forestall overconfidence among his supporters.

It was an absurd line clearly worked out by Gore and his campaign advisers after the news of the poll broke that morning. And the candidate was determinedly "on message." Watching from a picnic table where I was sitting with a couple of his consultants, I heard him repeat the line over and over again, almost word for word, time after time. Then he spotted me, an old acquaintance, and came over to shake hands. To my chagrin, he repeated the line to me, as if I had just fallen off the turnip truck that very morning. Al Gore is an intelligent man, but he was doing what he had been told would work. I tried to kid him out of it by pointing out I wasn't writing it all down, but he didn't get it.

Four years later I began to wonder if I had misjudged the appeal of this line when I heard Howard Dean saying with a straight face during the New Hampshire primary that he liked being behind because it got his troops all fired up. But Dean, unlike Gore, lost the primary by a wide margin. So much for the virtues of fighting uphill.

Increasingly, voters let the candidates get away with these campaigns that are hollow of content and almost totally contrived. More to the point, the voters allow the candidates and their handlers to set the agenda and define what a campaign is to be. And the press seems incapable of interceding in a way that makes any impression on the voters.

The ideal campaign sought by the handlers is one in which Americans cannot tell which television appearances are paid commercials and which are what the consultants call "free media" or "earned media," meaning news coverage. Ronald Reagan, running downhill for reelection in 1984, set the standard that October. His commercials depicted the candidate bathed in autumnal reds and golds. And the news stories showed him speaking from high school stages that had been decorated with corn husks, pumpkins, baskets of red and gold leaves, and barrels of apples. The message in both cases was that everything was grand.

Too often the candidates and their strategists rely on the most basic appeal to potential voters because they know they are probably not paying much attention and thus swallow whatever seems comfortable if they hear it often enough. It has always been called the Big Lie, and in the permissive context of American politics today, it works.

There are few examples more instructive than the tactic used by George W. Bush to salvage his campaign for the Republican presidential nomination in 2000. Bush had lost the New Hampshire primary to Senator John S. McCain of Arizona by 18 percent of the vote, a staggering margin in light of the fact that Bush had entered the campaign as a prohibitive favorite.

But McCain had offered himself as an engaging fresh face conducting the kind of open campaign that has become so rare in American politics. In the eight months leading up to the primary, he rode his campaign bus, the Straight Talk Express, across the state and held 114

town meetings. His openness and his identification with political reform hit a nerve with voters that overwhelmed even the intense support for Bush within the Republican establishment.

After the defeat, Bush and his advisers retired to Austin to devise a
new strategy. They were tough, tenacious, and still well funded, and
they were not about to yield to this maverick from Arizona. Their attitude for more than a year had been that this nomination belonged to
George W. Bush, and who was this interloper, anyway?

On Monday Bush stepped out of a telephone booth as a new candidate. What they had come up with was the ultimate use of the Big
Lie—a campaign in which the Texas governor claimed to be "A Reformer with Results." There was not a shred of evidence that Bush
ever reformed anything in his years as governor. In fact, the specifics
the campaign produced were full of holes. But his surrogates and
spokesmen hammered at the slogan relentlessly, day after day. When
Bush himself appeared, he was always standing in front of a blue cur-
tain bearing in silver letters the legend A REFORMER WITH RESULTS. If
some local reporter wanted to ask him about it, that was okay, too.

There was nothing subtle about the Bush message. The inference
you were supposed to draw was clear: This guy McCain may claim to
be a reformer, but he's never accomplished anything and I have, so
there.

It worked. The press did some small-bore carping about the lack of
supporting evidence, but the mainstream press was too grand to spend
its attention quibbling with a slogan. And the voters could hardly be
expected to pay enough attention to recognize the lie. So, after ten
days without serious challenge to the notion of Bush the reformer,
both the Bush and McCain campaigns found Republican-primary
voters about equally divided on which of their two candidates deserved
the identification. There were other factors involved in McCain's ultimate loss of the nomination, but the muddying of his clear reputation
as a reformer was a serious one.

The Republicans do not have a monopoly on such venal politics.
And there are Republican professionals and Republican candidates
who are unwilling to do anything it takes to get elected. The Demo-

crats, moreover, have some hacks of their own who are quite ready to do whatever it takes. It just seems that the Republicans are better at it. Democrats seem to feel there are limits on how far they can go before they provoke a backlash from their own side. Being a political liberal seems to entail, among other things, limiting the use of harsh tactics.

Campaigns have become mindless exercises played out for a few moments on the home screen. Most candidates and their managers seem to think the ultimate risk is to reveal your humanity. They are more comfortable with staged events they can control. And if the voters don't like it, they can just tune out.

Given the decline in participation, you might think the politicians would recognize that a different approach—such as John McCain's in New Hampshire—is worth trying. But politics is an imitative business, and it is success that is imitated, not a good showing. McCain, after all, lost in the end. So much for candor.

What works is what you can get on the television screens. If you give them circuses, perhaps people won't wonder where they might find the bread of substance.

3

EMPTY RITUALS

*I*f you ask Americans what a presidential campaign means to them, they may mention the national nominating conventions during the summer and the candidate debates in the fall. Both interfere with normal prime-time television schedules, a reasonably serious sin.

But the politicians themselves love rituals, and so does much of the press. So there is a certain amount of inertia in favor of the conventions even if it is not shared by the money managers of the television networks who have cut prime-time coverage to the bone. And the debates have become the main events of both the primary and general election schedules. As such, they are the subjects of intensive planning and scheming by the campaigns.

On paper, both the conventions and the debates would seem to offer opportunities to enlist the interest of potential voters who are turning away from American politics in such conspicuous numbers. The debates can produce at least the appearance of genuine drama. Those who saw it are not likely to forget Ronald Reagan in 1980, shaking his head in mock regret and saying to Jimmy Carter, "There you go again." Nor will they forget Lloyd Bentsen playing the "Jack

Kennedy was a friend of mine" card against Dan Quayle in the 1988 vice presidential debate.

By contrast, it is a rare moment indeed when anything memorable, let alone significant, happens at the national conventions these days. The citizen who spends convention week shooting grouse in Scotland hasn't missed anything. The choice of the nominee has been fore-ordained by the voters in state primaries and conventions, so the call of the roll of states is essentially ceremonial. And most often the nominee's pick for vice president has been announced well before the convention. The Big Story is the breathless minute-by-minute account— known in the trade as the "tick-tock"—of how the favored one was chosen and notified. Be still my heart.

The goal in this age of mechanistic politics is to avoid allowing any boomlets to develop about who should be on the ticket. No nominee wants a situation in which there are seven prominent party leaders who have been publicly disappointed and one ingrate. In any case, those controlling campaigns shudder at the notion of an unscripted moment. Who knows? Someone might say something controversial—or even interesting.

So the conventions have become such elaborately staged commercials for each party that the major broadcast networks are finding it easy to justify tuning them out for long stretches.

It can be argued, nonetheless, that the conventions are worth some attention from the press and the voters despite their failure to provide enough entertainment value to hold a television audience. They are an important if predictable part of the process of choosing a president and, as such, deserve to be documented by any news organization that takes itself seriously. Not everything has to be entertaining, after all. There is even the chance, slim though it may be, that "something will happen"—a surprising revolt against a vice presidential choice, per-haps, or an indiscreet remark by the nominee-presumptive, or a White House consultant getting caught fondling a prostitute while talking strategy on the telephone with the president.

There is always the chance, too, that some colorful and intriguing new players will emerge on the national political stage. Most Americans were given their first look at Governor Mario Cuomo of New York when his rhetoric transfixed the 1984 Democratic convention in San Francisco and the force of his personality filled television screens across the country. That speech made him a national figure overnight and would have made him a formidable contender for some future presidential nomination if he had ever been able to tear himself away from his strange attachment to Queens.

Two nights later at that same convention, the nation watched as Representative Geraldine Ferraro became the first woman named to either party's national ticket. If that didn't attract your interest, you should check your pulse. As she described it herself, "What a gas."

The conventions are also worth observing and reporting for what they tell us about the differences between the two parties. The Republicans are likely to be white, middle-class, suburban, and involved in small-business and family enterprises. In the last generation they also have become more likely to be religious fundamentalists primarily concerned with writing their "values" into the Republican platform. They have repeatedly put their party on record, for example, demanding that all judicial appointees oppose abortion rights. In 2000 they staged their convention in Philadelphia with blacks and Latinos conspicuously represented before the cameras as speakers and entertainers in a clumsy effort to suggest that the party isn't as white as it is. It was a joke.

The Democrats make a fetish of their diversity, and that, too, can be laughable. It is a rare moment when someone glancing at the podium won't see whites, blacks, and Latinos in roughly even numbers of men and women. There are disproportionate numbers of union members and academics. For the Democrats in particular, the convention serves a valuable purpose by throwing together delegates from, let's say, Maine and Louisiana so they discover the common things that bind them, when they are obviously as different as crayfish and lobsters.

Like the campaigns themselves, however, the conventions have been stripped of much of their color and texture by the planners' craze to avoid repeating the unhappy experiences of the past. Or, put another way, the conventions have been gelded so they cannot provide anything that might earn the attention of most Americans long enough for them to get caught up in the campaign. It was not always that way, however.

The Democrats have only recently begun to shake off the memories of the most tumultuous convention in their history—at Chicago in 1968. That was the year President Lyndon B. Johnson was forced to forgo a second term because of the volatility of the protests against the Vietnam War. Instead, the Democrats nominated Vice President Hubert H. Humphrey, who had sat out a searing primary struggle in which Robert F. Kennedy defeated Eugene J. McCarthy—and was immediately shot down at the Ambassador Hotel in Los Angeles.

By the time delegates gathered in Chicago, the party was in flames and thousands of antiwar demonstrators filled the city in protests that finally provoked what a subsequent investigation called "a police riot." Through their television sets, Americans were presented with the spectacle of a convention hall packed with Democratic leaders screaming obscenities at one another. After Humphrey suffered a narrow defeat at the hands of Richard M. Nixon, there was considerable evidence that the images projected by the turmoil in Chicago contributed to the defeat.

Nor was that 1968 convention the only one that has given the Democrats less of a campaign springboard than they might have wanted. In 1972 the struggle for small-*d* democratic reforms within the party process caused enough chaos in the Miami Beach convention hall that the nominee, Senator George S. McGovern of South Dakota, did not make it to the podium for his acceptance speech until after 2:00 A.M. eastern time. Again, it was not a pretty picture for the electorate at large, although many of the delegates who took part thought they had been involved in a demonstration of true democracy.

In 1980 President Jimmy Carter was assured of nomination at the New York convention but obliged to go through some awkward motions to project a picture of party unity with the man he defeated in the primaries, Senator Edward M. Kennedy. The lasting image from that one was Kennedy reeling around the podium while Carter tried to drag him into the traditional hands-clasped, arms-raised tableau of political unity.

The Republicans have lived through some less threatening but—for a party that puts a premium on following the regular order of things—still unsettling conventions. In Kansas City in 1976 Ronald Reagan came within a whisker of stealing the nomination from President Gerald R. Ford. Four years later, in Detroit, the party was embarrassed by an abortive attempt to install Ford as Reagan's running mate. At Houston in 1992 some Republicans high in the party structure were abashed at the prime-time attention given to the speeches of Patrick J. Buchanan and Marilyn Quayle.

Opinion polls show that the voters notice and disapprove of these untidy conventions. The Democrats paid a price in both 1968 and 1972, and it is part of Republican lore that the Reagan challenge in 1976 was the reason Ford lost so narrowly to Carter in November. So the impetus among both Democrats and Republicans has been to hide any differences under displays of patriotism and party fervor.

Conventions are the ultimate hothouses in which the acorn of a rumor at breakfast can become a full-size oak by lunch. In days past, the first imperative for a reporter covering a convention was always to avoid being conned into believing some bizarre story just because it was being repeated so often. Now the events are all so rigidly programmed that reporters seeking something that will qualify as news are forced to cover such momentous issues as whether the Democrats will allow the whining loser Jerry Brown to speak in prime time (no) or whether black musicians will outnumber black delegates at the Republican event (yes).

In contrast with conventions, debates have all the elements of a good story for the press—high stakes, direct confrontation, winners and losers. As hard as they try, the campaign strategists cannot wring out the last drops of emotion and uncertainty. The candidates usually are prideful men—or women, lately—who want to beat the other guy. If they have reached the point of running for president—or, for that matter, a Senate seat or governorship—they are likely to be intensely competitive as well as tenacious.

The most memorable debates, however, are those recalled for the gaffe someone committed—or, less often, for the riposte that would be repeated endlessly by the television networks. That is precisely what happened in that Bentsen-Quayle meeting in 1988. Quayle, seeking to reinforce his credentials as a senator from Indiana, compared his experience in the Senate with that of John F. Kennedy before he was elected to the White House in 1960. Bentsen, although he never acknowledged as much in so many words, had been prepared during predebate rehearsals for just such a moment.

"Senator, I served with Jack Kennedy," he said, with scorn and condescension. "I knew Jack Kennedy. Jack Kennedy was a friend of mine, and Senator, you are no Jack Kennedy."

Quayle was devastated. He finally muttered, "That was really uncalled-for, Senator."

But Bentsen would not back away. "You are the one that was making the comparison, Senator," he went on, "and I'm the one who knew him well. And frankly, I think you are so apart in the objectives you choose for our country that I didn't think the comparison was well-taken."

It was a moment in debate history that has been stamped indelibly on the consciousness of the political world. And one that fixed the perceptions of both men. It killed any vague hope Quayle might have nourished that he could overcome his reputation as a clueless lightweight—a reputation that made his comeback attempt in 2000 a hollow exercise. And it also gave a measure of vindication to Bentsen, the proud Texan who still smarted from the weak campaign he had run for the presidential nomination twelve years earlier. Democrats began talking about how the ticket should have been reversed, with Bentsen on top, and when Bentsen appeared at a rally outside Philadelphia, the band played the theme from *Rocky*.

None of this had anything to do with whether Dan Quayle might be qualified for vice president, of course, but that kind of question is beside the point when the press and political community are writing their reviews of a debate. For some essentially inexplicable reason, it has become the norm to view these events as theater and judge them on their entertainment value. There is apparently no crime more serious than boring the television audience.

Those reviews are important, nonetheless, because they influence the first returns in the popular verdict on who won or lost. The first polling on the debate between President Gerald Ford and challenger Jimmy Carter in 1976, conducted the same night as the debate in the earlier, eastern time zone, showed an edge for the Republican incumbent. But when the survey moved across the country the next day, the figures swung decidedly to Carter. The difference was that these later respondents had been told by pundits on television or by stories in newspapers about Ford's gaffe—an erroneous and baffling claim that Poland was not under the domination of the Soviet Union.

The press never fully explained how Ford made this mistake. He was neither so stupid nor so unschooled in foreign affairs that he didn't understand the relationship between the Soviets and the rest of Eastern Europe. He knew better—there were six Soviet divisions in Poland at the time—but inexplicably refused to back away from his assertion until a two-day controversy forced him to realize the trouble he had caused for himself. But you might have inferred from the furor about the gaffe that the president had effectively disqualified himself from ever entering the Oval Office again.

Whatever the hazards for the candidates, the presidential debates have become institutionalized over the last several presidential-campaign cycles. In theory, a candidate could refuse to take part. An incumbent president facing a silver-tongued challenger, for example, might plead that national security could be endangered. But the political cost of ducking a debate would be high enough so even that golden excuse wouldn't work.

In fact, the institutionalization of the debates is a mixed blessing. It does mean that there will be at least a couple of occasions in which the American people can compare directly those who want to be president. And the figures for the audiences are impressive.

The candidates use the debates largely to repeat their standard campaign speeches, which is something voters should hear but not the only criterion on which to make a decision. It is just as important, for example, for the voter to take some measure of the personality, style, and gravitas of the two candidates. Are they heavy enough for the White

House? Can anyone so dull lead the country? Can anyone so glib be genuine? Can a potential voter make a judgment based on one or two ninety-minute television shows?

Often the critical moment is the one in which, like Gerald Ford, the candidate commits a gaffe that then grows all out of proportion to its importance in judging a possible president.

Four years later it was Carter's turn. He dealt with a question on national-security policy by telling the audience that his twelve-year-old daughter, Amy, was "very concerned about nuclear proliferation." The howls of derision went on for several days as the remark was televised over and over again. In the three days after that debate, I heard Americans in cities as diverse as Tampa and Philadelphia making fun of Carter for "that thing about Amy and the bomb," as one Floridian put it.

The classic stumble probably came in 1992 when President George H. W. Bush, clearly uneasy in handling questions about the parlous condition of the economy, was caught looking at his watch while challenger Bill Clinton provided a reassuring answer to a questioner. You could make a case that the election was decided in that picture of a sitting president out of touch and out of sorts. But when an incumbent wins only 38 percent of the vote, there are always many turning points.

The debates, like so many other elements of American politics, have been distorted and cheapened by the consultants and strategists trying to make their candidate "the winner"—and by the press in aiding and abetting this ridiculous process.

In the 1960s and 1970s, when televised debates were first becoming a part of most campaigns, both sides made vigorous efforts to persuade the jurors of the press that their candidates had won. Often the candidates themselves would join in this rudimentary campaign to "spin" the press by holding a quick news conference.

But the politicians decided that if a little spin was good, overkill was better. Things reached the point in the last two or three cycles at which written talking points—one candidate's flacks attacking the other candidates—were delivered to the reporters watching in the pressroom while the debate was still going on. And once it ended, dozens of surrogates would flood the room, marching up and down the aisles between press tables and computers, offering themselves for instant quotations and expert analysis. (I enjoyed a delicious moment in 1992 when John Sununu, White House chief of staff under Bush, stopped in front of my computer to offer his goods as I was writing my story for the Baltimore *Sun*. When he started explaining how Bush had won, I stopped him. "John," I said, "you've been refusing to return my telephone calls for four years, and now you want me to listen?" Journalistic purists may say refusing to listen to the White House chief of staff was unprofessional. But I'm not a purist, and the chance to take a cheap shot was too good. The rule in Washington is: What goes around comes around.)

Moreover, thanks to the craven press, these spin tactics worked. Reporters were not only listening to the spin but going out in search of it. They were, in effect, seeking out people to lie to them so they could pass it on to the readers and viewers as opinion on the debate worth reading or seeing. By the time Clinton was running for reelection, the debate pressroom had become such a madhouse that his campaign sent its surrogates out with young handlers holding signs above their heads reading, for example, SECRETARY OF LABOR or SECRETARY OF AGRICULTURE. Reporters now could be selective in where they took their spin.

It is, of course, just the kind of thing that produces dull stories with little to interest readers or viewers. If John Sununu was admitting that Bush had had a disastrous debate, it would qualify as news. But John Sununu praising Bush to the skies would be easy to ignore.

In the case of the debates, however, at least it could be said that the voters were being offered some raw material that could be the basis for a decision on a candidate. And occasionally there might even be a surprise that would illustrate the power of a debate.

In 1980 John B. Anderson, a Republican congressman from Illinois, ran for president as an independent after earning a reputation in the primaries as a freethinking and outspoken candidate. I wrote a column describing the typical Anderson supporter as a member of the

League of Women Voters who lived in the suburbs, drove a Volvo, thought wine-and-cheese parties were fun, and ate the prune Danish on purpose when she went to a coffee.

I soon received a letter from a woman who had seen the column in the Portland *Oregonian* and wanted to ask: "Do you know me?" It turned out she fit all my specifications except for liking prune Danish. And she and about twenty other LWV women were meeting frequently to discuss the campaign. Most of them were Republicans, she said, but unwilling to commit themselves to Reagan, whom they considered dangerous. They were divided about evenly between Carter and Anderson.

In September Anderson continued to hold about 20 percent of the vote in the national polls and was invited to Baltimore to debate Carter and Reagan. But Carter, using some trumped-up excuse to avoid calling even more attention to Anderson, refused to debate.

So Anderson and Reagan squared off in a ninety-minute debate that was spirited without being unpleasant. If one of them won on points because of his superior knowledge of the issues, it was probably Anderson. But when I called my Anderson supporter in Oregon, I found that most of the Republican women had switched to Reagan. He might not have been clearly superior to Anderson on issues, but Reagan had been adequate and, at the least, nobody to fear. And, more to the point, good enough so there was no reason to waste a vote on an independent.

Over the next few days the same phenomenon showed itself nationally. Anderson lost about half his support as Republicans decided they could abide Ronald Reagan after all. After the campaign the Reagan strategists were convinced the debate with Anderson was a critical turning point in his triumph over the reputation he enjoyed as, in his words, "a combination of Ebenezer Scrooge and the Mad Bomber."

Peter Hart, a pollster and respected veteran of the political wars, likes to say: "The public only opens a window at certain times, and that's why debates are so important." I wouldn't quarrel with that analysis. But being important or even influential doesn't mean debates are edifying or, in the end, a sound basis for choosing a president.

4

FAIRNESS OR A REASONABLE FACSIMILE THEREOF?

*W*hen John Edwards made the formal announcement of his candidacy for the Democratic presidential nomination in 2004, *The Washington Post* published an eighteen-paragraph story describing the setting in Robbins, North Carolina, and what he had to say. Then, in the tenth paragraph, the story read: "Republican National Committee spokeswoman Christine Iverson dismissed his candidacy today, saying that nine months of campaigning and a recent advertising campaign in Iowa and New Hampshire have done little to boost his standing. Then, referring to an Edwards television appearance Monday night, she said, 'Maybe that's why he announced his candidacy on Comedy Central.' "

A thoughtful reader might wonder why in the world the opinion of a partisan hired gun was included in this otherwise innocuous account of a candidate declaring his intentions. If a spokeswoman for the Republican Party had said something positive about the Democratic senator and prospective presidential candidate, that would have qualified as news. But just another wisecrack? Who could possibly care?

he sometimes strange world of political journalism, the test is not just whether something is newsworthy. It is also whether it contributes to the perception of fairness on the part of the newspaper. Editors like to hear "all sides" of every story even when there is only one.

Reporters have a particular weakness for the "good quote"—usually meaning something clever or cogent—but the important thing is who is being quoted. If this is a Democrat running for president, it has to be a Republican even if the "good quote" is puerile. So all through the preliminaries to the 2004 campaign, close readers of political news were treated to quotes from totally obscure people like Christine Iverson. No one should be surprised if those readers move on to some other story.

News organizations, both print and electronic, have always had an awkward problem either being absolutely fair or at least giving that impression to the public. With television, the Federal Communications Commission supposedly addressed this dilemma by requiring that all candidates receive equal time. This notion is, of course, a joke. Anyone who believes fairness can be assured by the amount of time devoted to a campaign or candidate underestimates the cleverness of television correspondents and news directors.

With a few exceptions, news organizations give lip service to their commitment to fairness in their political coverage. Their failure lies in how they define it. Too often their idea of fairness is too unsophisticated. They want to project the appearance of fairness without coming to grips with the complex questions that arise in politics. In the case of newspapers, we have too many editors who really don't edit. Rather than dealing with vexing questions about what qualifies as news, they follow "rules" they learned from previous generations of editors equally well-intentioned but also equally superficial. It is always easier to just quote someone from "the other side" even if the story is intrinsically one without two sides.

Some newspapers seem to think they are being fair if they give the same amount of attention to both sides in terms of space or "play"— meaning positioning of a story; are they both on page one, or inside the paper, or, in the time-honored phrase, "back with the truss ads"?

There have been some editors so unsure of their own judgment that they actually used yardsticks to measure the column inches given each side. A few newspapers justified their claim to fairness by providing what were called "battle pages"—space devoted in equal amounts to statements from competing campaigns. Nobody would read the stuff, but nobody could complain either.

These days the standard that requires the least agonized decision making by editors is one that quotes someone with credentials, on paper anyway, as a neutral expert. That is why you so often see political scientists being quoted by political reporters who themselves are experts on the subject. The theory is that the reader or viewer will be reassured by the imprimatur of academic expertise—even in cases in which the reporter knows far more than the person being quoted.

For three golden years I worked for an editor at the *Washington Star,* James Bellows, who was confident enough in his own judgment and mine that he didn't play that game. If I knew enough about a story, I could write about the significance of some development under the "news analysis" heading without calling up some professor available by the mouthful to provide some cover in the form of quotes and a "source." As it turned out, no one was outraged. We got away with it without readers getting exercised and without being unfair to anyone. But Bellows was an editor without peer in my experience.

At all levels, the fairness question is the one that drives news executives to distraction. Covering the Middle East, they are certain to be accused by some Jews of being anti-Israel and by some Arabs of being in the hire of the Zionists. Writing about local affairs, they are inevitably charged with favoring the business community and the advertisers to protect profits. Writing about national politics, newspapers are just as inevitably accused of leaning either Republican or Democratic, depending on who is doing the leaning.

The critics see conspiracies to keep the truth under cover on every page. And although those notions may be fanciful, they persist because few laypeople have any idea how things work in news operations and even fewer appear to have any interest in finding out. They are reluctant to accept that things they see as the products of conspiracies are usually only unfortunate mistakes made in the very hectic business of putting out a newspaper or a television-news broadcast. Nor will they believe that when it comes to who wins what, most of the reporters and editors don't really give a damn—or at least enough of a damn to join in some arcane plot to deceive the public.

Some blame the publishers, those fat cats in their executive suites, for ordering the line the coverage should take. There was a time when there were some newspapers where that apparently was true—the Indianapolis newspapers under Eugene Pulliam and the *Chicago Tribune* under Bertie McCormick were always the ones being accused of a right-wing bias that was evident in news coverage.

These days, however, with a few exceptions newspaper publishers are like aging Mafia dons in their quest for respectability. They want the good opinion of others in the news community. And they don't want to take the chance of some underpaid reporter getting huffy and calling the Ethics Police.

Moreover, most newspapers are publicly held these days and cannot risk a bad reputation that might adversely affect the price of the stock. Too often, when the choice is between readers and stockholders, readers get the short straw, although no one in the newspaper business will admit it on pain of excommunication.

The other familiar accusation from the great uninformed is that a newspaper's news coverage reflects its editorial pages. To those in the business, that is particularly laughable. In any newspaper of even modest pretensions, the line between editorials and news stories is clearly defined. Most reporters know who is writing the editorials and are inclined to think of them as unfortunate people who have been forced to stay in the office because their legs have given out. That is not always either fair or accurate in describing editorial writers, but it is a view widely shared in newsrooms. Many reporters, myself included, rarely read editorials except in those occasional cases when they become factors in a political situation.

Bill Ringle, one of the very best reporters I have ever known, once did a brief stint as an editor of a small Gannett newspaper in Saratoga Springs, New York, and was asked at an editors' conference how he found writing editorials. He replied that it was a lot easier than being a reporter and having to dig out the facts of the stories on which editorials are based. This didn't satisfy his listeners, most of them editorial writers themselves, and they persisted until he finally replied: "Writing editorials is like wetting your pants in a blue serge suit. It gives you a nice warm feeling and nobody notices." That seemed to exhaust their interest in the topic.

We should not, however, equate a lack of partisan bias in news coverage with intelligence, acuity, and professionalism. The truth, a hard one to acknowledge if you have spent your life in the business, is that the coverage is often unfair to the politicians and mindless enough to discourage the interest of casual readers and viewers who should be voting in greater numbers. It contributes substantially to the level of ignorance and naïveté about public policy and politics and leaves openings for the braying jackasses on radio and cable television.

The coverage of presidential campaigns, ostensibly the most important, is particularly mindless. In most campaigns for, let's say, the Senate or a governorship, reporters get to know the candidates reasonably well and have the opportunity to learn—and pass on to readers or viewers—why they are doing whatever they are doing. And the more information reporters have, the easier it becomes to be truly fair in covering politics.

At the presidential level, by contrast, the principals have been carefully cosseted and isolated—apparently because of fear among their handlers that they might show some small touch of humanity, heaven forbid. So reporters are left to quote the flacks for each candidate attacking the other day after day. But if editors were to be genuinely fair to readers, they would assign a far lower value to these essentially ersatz stories that are nothing but exchanges of taunts. Instead, the basic criterion for fairness is too often whether our handling of a story will forestall complaints from partisans on one side or the other. That is neither reporting nor editing. It is covering your ass.

The willingness of the news media to accept these crumbs serves another purpose for the campaign strategists who know how much voters dislike negative politics. Faceless campaign "officials" do the dirty work. And on the rare occasion when the candidate can be asked about something rotten one of his advisers said, he can shake his head in mock regret and note that he himself wouldn't have put it that way. That wasn't George W. Bush who said John McCain ignored the needs of veterans; that was just some staff hack or some old guy from a veterans' organization. The voters, paying little attention anyway, are willing to swallow that because they already know politics is a dirty business. It is what they have come to expect and one of the reasons they turn a deaf ear to politics so much of the time.

This is not the only way in which the campaign operatives control the agenda followed by the news media. The starting point for reporters assigned to a campaign is always the candidate's daily schedule. The television reporters are looking for events that will provide the kind of pictures on which their medium feeds so voraciously. The newspaper reporters are looking for events that will bring them close to the candidate and perhaps even to the interaction between the candidate and some voters. Both are looking for that most elusive commodity, the real story about What's Going On.

It is true, of course, that major newspapers and the television networks don't limit themselves to trailing around after the candidates. Both do more complex stories about issues, trends, and anomalies. But, especially on television, the story that gets the most attention is the one where the candidate is shown saying something, preferably against an attractive backdrop like a mountain range or an ocean. Good visuals. Never mind what he is saying.

As a practical matter, most of what candidates do in presidential campaigns these days is irrelevant in terms of its impact on the electorate. Very few voters ever see the candidates in the flesh. All that matters most days is what they see on the evening news broadcasts on ABC, CBS, and NBC. Those reports and the television commercials are the basic diet of politics for most voters or potential voters. And they also provide the grist for the mills of the talk shows that run Sunday mornings on the networks and almost endlessly on the cable outlets.

For serious print reporters the broadcasts are also must viewing because they are the one way the reporters can find out what most Americans are learning about the story they are covering. For any newspaperman with normal professional pride, that is a hard concession to make—but one most of us choked down long ago.

For the political press, however, the true gold is the controversy, real or imagined, centered on which campaigns may be "in trouble" or "spinning out of control" or "struggling uphill." In many cases these stories follow a familiar pattern as more and more detail is uncovered by the dogged reporters and the pressure begins to build on the candidate to either provide an explanation that ends the controversy or get out of the campaign.

What is too often lacking, however, is a thoughtful decision by the press on the fairness of the story, not just the appearance of fairness. Two stories involving Gary Hart make the point in stark terms and suggest how fairness or the lack of fairness can affect a political outcome, particularly when voters are unwilling to pay close attention.

The first was the Donna Rice episode that destroyed Hart's candidacy in 1987. Once *The Miami Herald* reported that the comely blonde had spent the weekend with the Colorado senator at a townhouse on Capitol Hill, it was just a matter of time before he was forced out of the competition he had been clearly leading for the 1988 Democratic nomination.

This was a case in which newspaper editors fulfilled their responsibility to examine the fairness of what we were doing or would be doing in pursuing the matter. There was a great deal of breast-beating by a few stuffy editors and columnists about the ethics of "hiding in the bushes" to catch Hart coming out of his townhouse with the blonde. The hypocrisy quotient was high, given the things that reporters often do, with their editors' blessing, to get a story—things like impersonating a cop or a welfare recipient or a close friend of the deceased. Let's face it, we've all done things we might find difficult to explain to our children.

In this case Hart himself invited the trouble and there was ample justification for breaking the story. As a campaign manager for George McGovern in 1972 and on other occasions, Hart had established a reputation within the political community for womanizing. And some of the "little stories" about him had begun to make their way into print. Indeed, it had reached such a point that when he began his second campaign for the White House in 1987, Hart's first imperative was to deal with the womanizing issue once and for all.

Once the Donna Rice story broke, it was only a matter of days. No politician could survive a picture of himself with a blonde on his lap on the deck of a boat called the *Monkey Business* docked in Bimini. It doesn't get much better than that, so it was no surprise when, only two weeks later, Hart scuttled his campaign—at a time when he had been the clear favorite to win the nomination and at least an even bet in the general election.

Hart always thought he was treated unfairly. But his dalliance with Rice when the ultimate prize was so near was seen throughout the political world—correctly—as evidence of personal hubris and political carelessness. He apparently had forgotten that a candidate for president has an obligation to those who have put him in that position and to his party. Veteran Democrats speculated about how much worse it would have been if the story had broken after Hart won the nomination and it was too late for the Democrats to make a correction.

There was, however, a special irony in the fate that brought Hart down in the 1988 campaign. Four years earlier, in his first quest for the Democratic nomination, he had been defeated by the kind of trivial controversy the press cannot leave alone—and that, in that case, did not accord the candidate the fair treatment he deserved.

In that campaign Hart and Walter F. Mondale, the former vice president, approached the final critical primaries in California and New Jersey after a back-and-forth contest that had been running through the winter and spring. Moreover, ten days out from those final primaries, it appeared that Hart might win.

The senator from Colorado was clearly ahead in California, where his relative youth and commitment to international economic growth and high technology gave him a pronounced advantage over the candidate favored by Big Labor and the old party establishment. But Mondale could afford to lose most of the California delegates so long as he won in New Jersey, where he enjoyed the backing of both the union and party leaders.

Hart, however, was gaining steadily in New Jersey on the strength of a television campaign designed by consultant Ray Strother to play on the pride among Jersey voters in the state's recent economic gains, particularly in high-tech industry. Then Hart made what proved to be a politically fatal mistake. Describing how he and his wife, Lee, divided their campaign duties, he told a small group at a Bel Air fund-raiser: "The deal is that we campaign separately. That's the bad news. The good news for her is that she campaigns in California and I campaign in New Jersey." When Lee noted that she had been given a chance to hold a koala bear, Hart responded: "I won't tell you what I got to hold—samples from a toxic dump."

It was the kind of small joke anyone might make in those circumstances. The only thing noteworthy about it was that Hart so rarely showed any sense of humor. In this case, there were reporters at the event and it proved to be a disaster. The "Jersey joke," as it became known, was the top of the campaign news on page one of the major newspapers in New Jersey, a state in which the newspapers are particularly important because there is no local television.

Any pretext of fairness in news coverage went over the side. All Hart had done was make the kind of wisecrack about New Jersey that its own citizens make all the time. Why was it now the lead story? Why did we pay so much attention to Mondale's crocodile tears about what an insult it had been and how Hart now should come to Jersey and apologize and agree to a debate? Hart was bleeding. His "Jersey on the march" television commercials suddenly sounded like an apology from a candidate who had made a wisecrack that went beyond the pale.

The inference you would draw from the coverage was that thin-skinned Jersey voters could not abide anyone mentioning there were some toxic wastes—a lot of toxic wastes, in fact—in their state. From any distance, the controversy that raged for several days seems ridiculous. But the media, newspapers and television alike, loves to find someone committing a gaffe and thus being in the awkward position of having to explain. In that case, the explanation didn't take and Mondale won the primary he had to win to claim enough delegates for the nomination.

In this instance, as in many, it would be impossible for the press to claim fairness or even a sense of adult responsibility to readers and viewers who might one day be voters.

What the press doesn't like to confront is its penchant for treating as news any minor gaffe, misstatement, or change of mind committed by a candidate. Changing your mind is a particular sin that leads to accusations of "flip-flopping" on the issues. According to this unwritten code, there is no room for anything but a perfect performance at all times. The question of what constitutes legitimate news is left unanswered. The question of what should constitute fairness is similarly ignored much of the time.

This focus on trivia bears high costs. For one thing, it makes some candidates so cautious that they can never relax and show some sign of humanity. It encourages the handlers—the consultants and staff—to be even more protective. We have reached the ridiculous point at which the press secretaries for members of the House of Representatives want to know what you want to question their tigers about should they return your call. (I like to say, "The White Sox chances" and see if anyone gets it.)

Finally, some prospective voters surely are turned away from politics by all the attention paid to things that, first, have nothing to do with their lives and, second, tell them nothing about how a candidate might perform once in office. The press may be fair by its own narrow definition, but no one could argue it is informative.

5

A CONFESSED LIBERAL

*W*hen someone, usually a suspicious conservative, asks me if it isn't true that most reporters are liberals, I confess: Sure they are. So what?

It is an answer that usually stops the inquisitor cold; most people are nice enough that they don't want to accuse you to your face of slanting the news. But the whole topic disconcerts some of my colleagues and friends who cover politics, and it makes editors uneasy. They are more comfortable with the kind of reply a politician might give—all about how labels don't matter, and how we never think about such things as we go our merry way, being objective and evenhanded in covering the news.

That's the kind of defense I used to offer. But I have learned that such a reply is so obviously baloney that no perceptive newspaper reader or television viewer is going to take it seriously. And to the extent that they don't, they are less inclined to pay attention to what we tell them about other things. In short, such denials are counterproductive. After all, these are the people we are trying to reach.

As a practical matter, I can't prove that most reporters are liberal, and neither can anyone else. Some self-ordained critic of the press did a survey a few years ago in which 85 percent of Washington correspondents in the sample admitted to voting for Bill Clinton over George H. W. Bush in 1992. The press haters of the far right have been crowing about it ever since. They finally have the proof of what they have been saying all along.

I doubt, however, that many reporters in my set agreed to take part in that survey. And besides, you didn't have to be a liberal to prefer Clinton to Bush. All you had to be was aware of what was going on around you. It was no accident that Bush took only 38 percent of the vote in 1992, a remarkably weak showing for an incumbent who was nice to his grandchildren and had committed no felonies in the Oval Office of which we are aware.

My generalization about reporters is based on the recognition that they—or at least those of my generation—have had much the same life experiences as I have had as a reporter. We didn't start out in our work lives as Washington correspondents or columnists or national political reporters. In my case, I spent a decade covering subjects as diverse as labor, organized crime, and urban renewal (then called "slum clearance") as well as local and state government and politics.

So over the years our work has exposed us to every part of the country and every level of society. We have seen at close range who is being left out, and we see an essential role for government to make the corrections so obviously needed. We cannot explain away the shabby treatment this rich society gives to so many children and old people who don't share the wealth. That is one of the criteria for defining a liberal—someone who expects government to play a role in resolving inequities, not just collect taxes and fight wars.

But the question to ask of a political reporter is not which label he will accept. Instead, it is whether being a liberal—or, just as commonly these days, a conservative—limits his ability to report accurately on the political campaign at hand.

Most of the stories involved in covering a campaign don't have any ideological content. As a result, my old and dear friend Bob Novak and

I often reach the same conclusions about a political situation, even though we stand at opposite poles on the issue involved. Being a liberal or a conservative doesn't interfere with reading poll results. Nor does it prevent you from understanding why a candidate starts ranting about abortion and demanding prayer in the public schools. He is a right-winger playing to his base.

Some critics of the media keep finding evidence of cabals among reporters and editors to promote their personal leanings in their coverage. However, in more than forty years of covering national politics, including thousands of dinners and hundreds of nights drinking with other reporters, I cannot recall a single conversation about our own ideology. Nor, for that matter, did I ever learn for whom any of us intended to vote, although someone eavesdropping on our conversations might have been able to make some accurate inferences.

We discuss the candidates and their advisers endlessly but rarely in terms of their ideological leanings. Instead, the conversation is more basic. Can you believe someone that dumb can become president? Have you ever seen such a stiff succeed in politics? Who told that guy to defend abortion rights at a Catholic hospital? Who's posing as another Kennedy or another Eisenhower? What a hoot. He's pretending to be John Wayne; he doesn't realize John Wayne wasn't John Wayne either.

The widespread suspicion of political reporters leads to the notion that we have great influence on the outcome of elections. That is laughable. Just read the box scores. In not a single presidential election since 1960 has either the Republican or the Democratic Party ever nominated, let alone elected, the candidate I would have liked to see in the White House.

I would have preferred, to cite just a few instances, Adlai E. Stevenson to John F. Kennedy in 1960, Nelson A. Rockefeller to either Barry Goldwater in 1964 or Richard Nixon in 1968, Morris Udall to Jimmy Carter in 1976, Howard Baker to Ronald Reagan in 1980, and so on. (These were preferences, however, based not on particular issues so much as on the personal qualities of the individuals. I thought, for example, that the country would have done well to have someone in the

White House with Udall's self-deprecating wit and sense of the ridiculous to keep things in some relationship to reality.)

Some of these were close calls. I thought Carter was the most intelligent candidate I had ever covered and was a man with decent instincts that gave me high hopes for his presidency. I would have preferred Robert F. Kennedy to Hubert H. Humphrey in 1968 because I thought he promised the radical change the country needed. But who could not like Hubert Humphrey? Liking is not enough of a measuring stick, however. I liked Barry Goldwater but thought his presidency would have been a disaster. I liked Ronald Reagan and never agreed with him on anything.

My suspicion is that many of my colleagues were harboring similar feelings, but it simply never came up in the conversation. There were always too many funny stories to tell. So much for cabals.

In fact, if my personal preferences had a practical effect on my reporting, it was the opposite of what the suspicious right-wingers would expect. I often bent over backward to avoid favoring a candidate I liked. Walking the line was sometimes tricky, but that is what professional reporting is all about. It was difficult to maintain a proper detachment from a candidate as exciting as Bob Kennedy in 1968, so much so that one great reporter, Richard Harwood of *The Washington Post,* took himself off the assignment for a while.

To some degree, those print reporters who also appear on television—like myself—have been responsible for reinforcing the suspicion among readers and viewers. The panel shows such as *The McLaughlin Group, Inside Washington,* and *The Capital Gang* try to achieve balance by offering people of varied ideological stripe. When I started on *McLaughlin,* the panel was made up of two conservatives, Bob Novak and Pat Buchanan, and two liberals, Morton Kondracke, who later moved steadily to the right, and me. Over the years the cast changed, but the mix was about the same. The panel was necessarily made up largely of columnists because only someone writing a column had the freedom to express opinions as directly as the format required.

By contrast, *Washington Week in Review* on public television could use reporters because the producers believed they were performing an educational purpose and put a premium on exposition of the issues at the heart of the week's major news stories rather than on debate. (John McLaughlin insisted his program was performing a similar service, but those of us on the panel knew better.)

In terms of the changes in the media, the panel shows were models of intellectual argument, at least when compared with the explosion of political talk on cable television and radio. And here the conservatives have all the best of it. They are prominent on CNN, CNBC, and MSNBC and dominant on the Fox News Channel, Rupert Murdoch's contribution to the enlightenment of the masses.

The head man at FNC is the redoubtable Roger Ailes, whose long history as an adviser to Republican presidential candidates has been one success after another. He had the smarts to play off the suspicions of the viewers by offering the FNC version of the news as the "straight goods," by which they mean nonliberal. Thus the slogans repeated over and over on FNC—"We report, you decide" and "Your source for fair and balanced news."

This is a little disingenuous, since the dominant figures on FNC are people who have been outed as devout conservatives long ago—Brit Hume, Tony Snow (a White House speechwriter in the first Bush administration and Rush Limbaugh's stand-in on radio before he moved to his own radio program), and Fred Barnes, who is also executive editor of *The Weekly Standard,* the magazine funded by Rupert Murdoch and run by William Kristol, last seen as the right-hand man of Vice President Dan Quayle.

The conservatives also seem to have a strong, perhaps dominant position in several little magazines—the *Standard, The New Republic,* and *National Review*—whose only readers seem to be one another's staffs and political junkies. Some of those who write for these magazines and appear on obscure cable television imagine there is some influential intellectual debate under way in the capital.

That, however, is a conceit. The writers may be intellectual, but they are hardly influential; all they are really doing is taking in one another's washing. If you want to get a hearing from Congress, better enlist Rush Limbaugh and his legions of "Dittoheads." Just compare the ratings for the talk shows and the cable programs to see where the power lies in American politics.

It isn't difficult to see why conservatives dominate the talk shows and the little magazines—it's called moral certitude. They are so sure not only that they are right but that their opponents are wrong and, in many cases, morally corrupt. For some reason lost on me, the rise of conservatism has come hand in hand with an increase in the number of journalists who have gone public with their religious fundamentalism.

The nature of the debate among the politicians has followed a parallel course. In the days of Barry Goldwater, his admirers believed that the progressive Republicans who followed Nelson Rockefeller were wrong on the issues but still Republicans entitled to be heard within the party. These days the noisiest leaders of the far right—the Quayles, Dick Armeys, Newt Gingriches, Tom DeLays—seem to believe liberal political opponents have no "family values."

We are treated to Senator Rick Santorum of Pennsylvania braying about how "evil" had been cleansed from the Senate when a bill restricting abortion passed. It has never been made clear who chose any of these people as moral arbiters for our society. (Equally puzzling is how the voters of Pennsylvania experienced a mass dizzy spell on not just one but two election days, when they chose and then reelected Santorum.)

On the other hand, liberals by definition seem less positive about the rightness of their positions. Their ethic includes tolerance of other views, something that does not burden the Limbaughs or Santorums of the world. The difference is apparent, for example, in the language used to identify the two sides in the abortion-rights debate. The conservatives are "pro-life" and the liberals "pro-choice," a term that can imply a somewhat wishy-washy lack of certitude.

Whatever the reason, it has become clear that there is little demand for liberal talk-show hosts, on either radio or television. The listeners and viewers and many newspaper readers, as well, apparently want strong guidance in their lives. And what they don't want is someone telling them all about how on the one hand we have so-and-so, on the other we have such-and-such. There is, in short, no market for thoughtful agonizing over issues.

In the long run, the tone of the ideological debate these days is clearly one of the things that discourage Americans from taking an active part in politics. Most people don't feel strongly enough about issues to believe that those who disagree with them are evil. And the politicians who take such strong stands are telling a large share of their constituents—the 40 or 45 percent who voted for the other candidate—that they hold views that are morally indefensible.

In fact, there are few issues of public policy that have intrinsic moral content for everyone. Civil rights was one of them. So, for many people, was the war in Vietnam. For others, it may be the separation of church and state. Or abortion rights. Or gun control. Or the protection of the environment for future generations.

But it isn't easy for most of us to get emotionally caught up in an argument over the capital-gains tax rate or trade relations with Latin America or even Medicare reform. And it is these prosaic issues that most often occupy the workday of the Washington correspondent, liberal or conservative.

One of the reasons for the hostility toward many in the press is the modest celebrity that attaches to anyone who appears on television on a regular basis. If you are a newspaper reporter, you find that all of a sudden people who have never read a word of your work are calling you a great reporter or even, horrors, "a great journalist." It is heady stuff, and it is sometimes difficult to maintain your balance. Strangers, sometimes delightful young women but more often earnest college kids, solicit your autograph in airports. Lecture agents offer fat fees and first-class air travel for you to come speak to, for example, the sand-and-gravel folks.

You can also be a target of a lot of anger. Many Americans are frustrated by their inability to gain a hearing for their views beyond their own breakfast tables. So they react angrily when they turn on the television and see some fat bald guy shooting off his mouth on every topic imaginable. It leads to intemperate letters and even the occasional threatening telephone call, usually anonymous.

A generation ago the only celebrities in the newspaper business were a few major syndicated columnists. And some of them were not as famous as they imagined. One was Joseph Alsop, a columnist for *The Washington Post* and hundreds of other newspapers and a man of what might charitably be called supreme self-assurance.

Traveling with Nelson Rockefeller's brief campaign for president in 1968, Alsop joined two reporters for lunch at a brief stop in Meriden, Connecticut. We had also invited Jackie Robinson, who had been along on the trip as a celebrity supporter of Rockefeller. When we introduced the two, Robinson made it clear he didn't know who Alsop was when he asked, "And who do you write for?" Monumentally offended at being mistaken for just another scribbler, Alsop pretended he didn't know Jackie Robinson. It was a pose difficult to maintain for an hour as autograph seekers besieged Jackie at the luncheon table.

That kind of thing can't happen today. Thanks to television, every celebrity knows every other celebrity, liberal or conservative.

6

TV RULES! ALL HAIL TV!

*T*he morning after the 1972 Democratic presidential primary in California, the winning candidate, Senator George McGovern of South Dakota, scheduled the usual winner's press conference in a mezzanine meeting room at the Wilshire Hyatt House in Los Angeles.

Those of us covering the campaign were nonplussed to discover several rows of chairs pointing in one direction and eight or ten television cameras pointing the opposite way. The TV crews had decided, one of the cameramen told me, that they didn't want to shoot over the heads of the people asking the questions, so tough shit.

When McGovern arrived, however, he paused momentarily at the entrance, clearly a little puzzled, and then walked to take up a position directly in front of the reporters. The TV crews were obliged to turn their cameras and lights around. It was one of the reasons we ink-stained wretches harbored a secret liking for McGovern. Whatever else they might say about McGoo, he had his priorities straight.

Some of us understood, nonetheless, that the tide was running against us. Tom Ottenad of the *St. Louis Post-Dispatch,* one of the most perceptive of our number, muttered that "before it's over they [television] are going to turn us into props." He was right. It took a little time, almost thirty years, but television now dominates media coverage of political campaigns and, for that matter, much of the shape of government policy. A crisis is a crisis only when it appears on the home screen. If you are a starving African, your best chance for salvation lies in being discovered by CNN.

Along the way, those of us who cover politics slowly recognized how the balance of power and influence was changing. After the 1968 campaign we learned from Joe McGinnis's book *The Selling of the President* that Richard M. Nixon's first priority was getting a story about his campaign on the evening news broadcasts of the three networks every night. (I've always been a little puzzled about the "selling" part because Nixon entered the campaign with 43 percent of the voters behind him in opinion polls and won the election over Hubert H. Humphrey and George C. Wallace with that same 43 percent of the vote.)

Whatever the explanation, we understood when the time came to cover the 1972 campaign that watching the network news every evening was part of covering the story. A campaign or two later we also found that we had to watch local news coverage in primaries or key states in the general election because, for some unfathomable reason, it had larger audiences. Viewers apparently want to be kept up-to-date on every two-alarm fire and mom-and-pop murder as well as, of course, the weather.

The transfer of power from print to electronic media has not been entirely seamless. In the early 1950s, for example, newspaper reporters covering the Michigan state capitol in Lansing rebelled when the Detroit television stations started sending camera crews but no reporters to the press conferences of Governor G. Mennen "Soapy" Williams. So they started sprinkling profanity through their questions, as in: "Why in the hell are you going to do that goddamn thing, Governor?" And Williams went along with the program, giving such replies as "I'm doing this goddamn thing because it's necessary as hell."

Because the television of the time relied on film that had to be developed to be edited, the poachers lacked the ability (which they acquired later with the use of tape) to quickly remove the profanity. So the camera crews alone were a waste of time and the stations were obliged to send reporters along with them. These days, of course, they would just broadcast the profanity.

For over two decades, from the 1950s through the 1970s, television coverage of politics was extremely tentative and derivative despite many assets the networks could bring to bear. They employed some highly skilled and experienced reporters, many of them defectors fleeing the rotten pay of the wire services and most newspapers at the time. When I covered the White House briefly during the early days of the Nixon administration, for example, three of the best reporters on the beat were Richard Valeriani of NBC, Bob Pierpoint of CBS, and Herb Kaplow of ABC.

The networks also employed and used wisely some excellent political reporters during the seventies and eighties—men such as Ken Bode, Sander Vanocur, Bruce Morton, Jim Wooten, Roger Mudd, and Tom Pettit. Although not as narrowly focused as their counterparts at newspapers, these were reporters who kept up with politics and politicians four years around, even when there wasn't a national story on the griddle, and thus did their own reporting and built their own stables of sources.

They were also, incidentally, reporters with whom the newspaper political writers felt totally comfortable because, quite aside from being good company, they shared the same fund of political knowledge and many of the same sources. This wasn't the case with everyone in television. There were some excellent newspaper reporters who switched to TV and apparently decided they no longer had to keep up with all the details to get by in their brief appearances on camera. So they quit doing the intensive reporting that made them knowledgeable—and good company over a drink or dinner.

But whatever the quality of the television reporting, at least until the middle of the eighties the network-news executives were uneasy about making the judgment calls that lie at the heart of good political coverage. They didn't know then what we have learned since—that is, that they can get away with just about anything.

The result of their timidity was that they followed the lead of the newspapers. I can remember in the late seventies writing front-page stories for the late, lamented *Washington Star* about some previously ignored political trend and then watching the same story ripple through the three major networks over the next few days. It used to give me a nice smug feeling of superiority. The same was true, in spades, of the stories written by my competitor and friend David Broder of *The Washington Post,* although he never seemed smug. And finally, any such story in *The New York Times* by anyone was replicated by TV almost before the paper hit the doorstep. For the network executives based in New York, a story in the *Times* might as well have been chiseled in stone.

The networks' reliance on the judgments of others was apparent even in their decisions about how much money and staff to devote to political stories. None of them caught on to the pivotal importance of the Iowa precinct caucuses, for example, until the newspapers paid attention to Jimmy Carter's breakthrough there in 1976. But they moved with impressive force once they moved. Covering the Iowa story four years later, in 1980, CBS assigned so many people and bought so many telephone lines—more than two hundred—that the phone company had to make up a new three-digit exchange to serve them.

TV's influence and hubris also grew rapidly through the 1970s. In the late spring of 1979 I joined Barbara Walters as a panelist at the American Newspaper Publishers Association (now the Newspaper Association of America) annual convention at the Waldorf-Astoria. We were assigned to a marathon panel session in which we were to question a series of subjects as diverse as, to cite the most prominent, Jane Byrne, the newly elected mayor of Chicago, and Governor Richard Thornburgh of Pennsylvania, who had just presided over the nuclear accident at Three Mile Island.

When the tour de force was ended, Walters turned to me and, intending to be complimentary, said, "Jack, you ask such good questions. You should be in television." I explained lamely that newspaper reporters also ask questions and slipped away muttering to myself. But I guess you could say I took her advice when Broder and I started doing a gig on NBC's *Today* show a year later.

Drawing any cosmic conclusions from the rise of television news is tricky. It probably isn't fair to point out that as TV's role has grown ever more prominent, voter participation has declined. There are too many things that might have been responsible for this phenomenon, including the quality of the candidates. It had to take some Herculean effort of will for many Americans to vote for either George W. Bush or Al Gore. Ye gods.

But it is fair to say that the growing influence of television in covering politics has not been matched by a growing sophistication in dealing with the subject matter. The best political strategists know how to exploit the inherent weaknesses of television. And they operate on the assumption that the potential voters won't pay close attention to what they are doing so there are no serious risks in even the most shameless demagoguery.

Television has two vulnerabilities in covering politics. First and most obvious, it is above all a visual medium. So the campaign that provides the best pictures can get itself on the air and thus into the homes and consciousness of millions of Americans. But politics is at its core a contest of ideas, however crude they may seem at times, and that is a quality that cannot be captured on tape. The result is that those ideas are rarely impressed on many, or perhaps even most, viewers.

Second, television news is always in a hurry. The networks have so little time to give their reports that they are susceptible to the punchy one-liner or the riveting moment. They may prefer the good picture that tells the story, but lacking the visual, they'll find the clever wisecrack almost irresistible. Although newspapers often fall for the same kind of one-liners, they have the space to provide a context for them that is missing on the television screen. The "printheads," as some of the TV types began calling us twenty years ago, also could deal with the complexity of politics rarely covered by TV because of the airtime required. On the NBC *Nightly News* with Tom Brokaw, they trumpet as "in-depth" segments that run two or two and a half minutes. Any reporter or editor watching can find a dozen questions that have not been answered.

In a sense, television is held captive by the medium's understandable obsession with the "great picture" at the expense of nuance. Never was that more evident than in the demise of the campaign of Howard Dean early in 2004.

Despite his limited credentials as a political leader, Dean had captured the fancy of many Americans in 2003 with his angry assault on Bush's policy in going to war against Iraq. And Democratic Party activists had been intrigued by his success in using the Internet to raise $40 million—a staggering amount for a neophyte Democrat—and to reach potential supporters. He leaped to the head of the polls much as George W. Bush had done, for different reasons, four years earlier. He was heavily favored in both of the early tests, the Iowa precinct caucuses on January 19 and the New Hampshire primary eight days later.

But Dean collapsed in Iowa, finishing far behind both John Kerry and John Edwards with only 18 percent of the caucus vote. Then he compounded the felony by delivering what used to be called a "redfaced speech" but in this case became known as a primal scream, all of it captured, of course, on television. The film was so compelling that, by one count, it was shown on television almost seven hundred times in the eight days leading up to the primary in New Hampshire, where his poll numbers were plunging. The clear implication was that "the scream" had destroyed his candidacy.

That was not the case, however. Dean's demise was a product of that 18 percent performance. It was an unmistakable signal of early buyer's remorse among Democrats. Dean had not shown an ability to roll with the political punches once he became the front-runner, not surprising for a governor of Vermont in the big leagues for the first time. And many Democrats found him too acerbic, bordering on arrogant rather than likable. In short, he was not a candidate in whom they could put great confidence to carry out the first priority: defeating George W. Bush.

Moreover, it was obvious that there were comfortable alternatives. Kerry had overcome some early problems with his own campaign, and if Bush wanted to make the war the issue, he was offering a stunning contrast with his credentials from the war in Vietnam. As the wise guys put it, he didn't have to rent a flight suit to land on the deck of a carrier.

The bottom line is that when choosing a president, Americans are aware there is some risk involved. And the Democrats in the primary states decided Howard Dean was too risky. Television's focus on the scream was only fresh evidence reinforcing doubts that were there long before he uttered it that night in Des Moines.

Kerry's success in Iowa was only the first of a string of triumphs demonstrating that Democrats had reached a consensus that he was the prospective candidate with the best chance of defeating George W. Bush.

A classic case of the inherent flaws in TV coverage is the handling of a day that proved pivotal in the 1988 presidential campaign. Dukakis had flown into Chicago to deliver a lunchtime speech spelling out his views on the proper relationship between the United States and the Soviet Union. It was obviously a topic of the highest priority and deserved thorough coverage by anyone in the press claiming to be performing a serious public service.

But that afternoon Dukakis flew to Sterling Heights, Michigan, and was taken to a General Dynamics plant at which he put on a helmet and plunked himself down into an M-1 tank. The result was a picture of the candidate looking like Alfred E. Neumann and riding around in the tank while the soundtrack picked up the laughter of onlookers—a scene ludicrous enough that the Bush campaign seized on it for its own commercials. That night all three broadcast-television networks understandably carried the scene at length but, less understandably, brushed off the important foreign-policy speech with only brief mentions. By contrast, *The Washington Post* carried the picture but also printed more than a column about what Dukakis had said in Chicago, referring to the tank episode only in the twelfth paragraph.

One instructive example of how TV can influence or even control

the course of a campaign is the 1984 contest for the Democratic nomination between Walter F. Mondale and Gary Hart. Mondale had been
the prohibitive morning-line favorite for the nomination because he
had the paper credentials, the money, and the support of most of the
party establishment and Big Labor. He had been in the trenches a long
time and was both liked and respected by activist Democrats.

But Hart ran better than expected in the Iowa caucuses and then
upset Mondale by a wide margin in the New Hampshire primary—in
some measure because of a great hit on television the Saturday before
the primary. He was shown at a lumberjack competition, wearing jeans
and a checked shirt he had chosen for the occasion and hurling an axe
that buried itself in a tree. In fact, it was his second try. On his first attempt the axe hit the tree and fell to the ground, but happily for Hart,
the cameras had not been ready. So they caught only his success, providing a clip that ran over and over for the next three days. Even his
feminist New Hampshire campaign managers, Jeanne Shaheen (later
the governor) and Sue Casey (later a member of the city council in
Denver), admitted that women voters swooned in droves at their
macho candidate. What throwing an axe had to do with being president has never been explained.

Hart went on to win in several other states until the campaign
reached Super Tuesday in early March with Mondale clearly on the
ropes. There were nine events scheduled that day, primaries or caucuses in Florida, Georgia, Alabama, Massachusetts, Rhode Island,
Hawaii, Nevada, Oklahoma, and Washington State. They would
choose 511 of the 1,967 delegates needed to win the presidential nomination in Chicago. That was the Super part.

The Mondale strategists decided to concentrate on the three southern primaries, insisting these were the ones that mattered because they
would demonstrate that Hart's earlier success in New Hampshire,
Maine, and Vermont was just a regional phenomenon. Thus, in effect,
they were trying to make a virtue out of a necessity by conceding to
Hart both Massachusetts and Rhode Island, and leaving it up to supporters on the ground in the western caucuses. Those states were

brushed off as essentially meaningless because of television. They were in the wrong time zones to report results for the networks' half-hour election-night specials that would air on eastern time. So, the implication seemed to be, they didn't matter.

Mondale's managers also decided it was time to play the Jimmy Carter card for these southern voters. After months of minimizing his role as Carter's vice president and political ally, Mondale suddenly flew to Plains, Georgia, for what was advertised as an "old-fashioned barbecue with Jimmy and Rosalynn." It was, like so much in politics, a Potemkin Village event: the Mondales and Carters walking from the Carter home on Woodland Drive down Main Street to the barbecue at the railroad station, where they spoke to a thousand cheering supporters, ostensibly the Carters' neighbors.

It was clear, however, that the reporters alone outnumbered the people from Plains in the crowd. Instead of the local folks gathering to share some barbecue, there were busloads of union members brought in from Albany and Columbus and even Atlanta for the event. Once the cameras were turned off, they got back on their buses and went home. But the networks all filmed the great visual and, because it was a Saturday, ran it over and over again. The producers of the network evening news and morning shows don't seem to think something has been covered unless they use it on their own programs, so Saturday events often are shown repeatedly, a practice not lost on political strategists.

The television reporters who covered the event, like those of us writing for newspapers, understood the artificial quality of the story and could see the union caps and jackets worn by those purporting to be Jimmy Carter's neighbors. But their disclaimers were lost in the attention claimed by the pictures as Mondale and Carter spoke from the back of the ubiquitous flatbed truck. The story, if any southern primary voters cared, was that old Fritz and old Jimmy were still close.

Then, almost by accident, Mondale scored another coup on television with his "Where's the beef?" thrust at Hart in a debate in Atlanta the Sunday afternoon before primary day. For Mondale it was an outlet for his frustration over the praise Hart had been winning as a candidate of "new ideas." As Hart discussed his plans for economic policy, Mondale suddenly broke in.

"You know," he said, "when I hear your ideas, I'm reminded of that ad, 'Where's the beef?'"

The line was familiar because the commercial had been running heavily for weeks, although Mondale had never heard it until campaign manager Bob Beckel briefed him the day before the debate. So it was no surprise that the audience in the Fox Theater in Atlanta broke into applause and laughter—or that the networks had found their new favorite sound bite to be shown over and over in the thirty-six hours before the Super Tuesday voting.

In the strictest sense, the Mondale question was grossly unfair. If anything, Gary Hart had too many ideas on policy that he repeated at the drop of a question from a reporter or a voter. But there is no great demand for fairness in big-league politics. And everyone at that level knows a crack like "Where's the beef?" is made for television news.

Nor was the Hart of 1984 the kind of candidate who excelled at exchanges of one-liners. At dinner with several reporters after the debate that night in Atlanta, Hart sipped Irish whiskey and delivered some wisecracks of his own with Mondale as the target. Asked why he didn't use these ripostes on the air, he shrugged and said that he just never found the right opening. It is probably closer to the truth to say that Hart was too self-conscious to be comfortable swapping zingers on live television.

Two days later the Mondale operatives pulled off the most important coup of the campaign up to that point, and defined a new pecking order in the press corps. They convinced the networks—as well as some of the print press—that if Mondale won two of the three southern primaries, it was a victory for him and a defeat for Hart. They knew by that time that they were cooked in Florida but narrowly ahead in Georgia, where Mondale had influential black support, and Alabama, where John Glenn was diverting votes that might otherwise have gone to Hart.

The Mondale agents sold their line assiduously. The real test of

Super Tuesday, we were told over and over, would be the three southern primaries that would show if Hart's magic could travel beyond New England. The campaign also set up an elaborate primary-night rally in Washington, inviting all the prominent Mondale supporters in the capital to gather, enjoy a few drinks, and then, properly relaxed, vent their enthusiasm for the cameras. And when the results came in, that is just what they did.

On the face of it, Hart had a huge success that night. He defeated Mondale in Florida (39–36 percent), Massachusetts (39–26), and Rhode Island (45–35) and captured all four caucuses. Mondale carried Alabama (34–21 each for Hart and Glenn and 19 for Jackson) and Georgia (30–27 for Hart, 21 for Jackson, 18 for Glenn).

So Hart won seven of the nine contests and lost Georgia so narrowly that it was reasonable to surmise he would have won if Glenn had not been in the field or if he had made any effort at all to cut into the black vote. By any conventional political reckoning it was a big night for Hart, big enough that Mondale later confessed that he would have withdrawn from the campaign entirely if he had lost in Georgia.

That, however, was not the way it sounded when the networks went on the air with their "special reports" that night. NBC went live as Mondale was declaring victory and being boisterously cheered by his packed house in that hotel ballroom in Washington. The politically astute Tom Brokaw went the whole nine yards: "Walter Mondale, alive and well tonight in his race for the Democratic presidential nomination, thanking, as he put it, his friends in the South. And well he might, because they have kept him in this race tonight."

Then he ran down the results showing Hart winning Florida and Massachusetts and, "as expected," Rhode Island, while Mondale had won "a big victory" in Alabama. "So tonight Gary Hart wins three states, Walter Mondale wins two—two of the big southern states that he had to have to stay in this race." Never explained was how Alabama qualified as a "big" one and why Mondale's victory there compensated for his losses in Florida and Massachusetts.

Brokaw was not alone among television leading men who clearly had been preconditioned by the Mondale strategy. Roger Mudd con ducted an interview with Hart that sounded like he had lost sight of Massachusetts, Rhode Island, and all those caucus states. When Hart recapitulated his successes, Mudd interjected: "But you didn't win in Georgia and you didn't win in Alabama, so really all you won was Florida, which isn't a true southern state. So you're really not a national candidate yet, are you?" Hart demurred, but that is not the kind of confrontation a politician can win. (Long after the fact, Mudd, a reporter with a reputation for fairness who had covered many big stories, conceded that that was one he regretted.)

Neither Dan Rather of CBS nor Peter Jennings of ABC was as totally entranced as NBC had been, but they also bought the Mondale line that his candidacy had been saved by those two states. Jennings even seemed somewhat abashed at what was happening while helping it along. "I was just thinking," he said at one point, "that if you'd arrived in this country tonight from outer space, you would have thought Hart was the big winner. Two states, two biggest states, Massachusetts and Florida. But because Walter Mondale set so many of the expectations for the South tonight, it looks, as I think we're pretty well describing it, as pretty much of a standoff."

Translated, Jennings seemed to be saying that Mondale had lost, but that because he warned us in advance about how weak Mondale was, it came out as a "standoff." Or, in other words, we bought it and we're sticking with it.

The one clear message was that the television networks had reached the point at which they made their own judgments and the rest of us should recognize we were obliged to go along. The morning after the primaries, David Broder and I made our usual appearance on the *Today* show and, to the chagrin of the producers, called the whole thing essentially a big win for Hart that left Mondale down to his last match. And we both took that tack in writing for our newspapers. But compared with the television networks, the influence of newspapers—even *The Washington Post*—was exposed as marginal at best.

Since that turning point two decades ago, the primacy of television in its reach with potential voters has grown in leaps and bounds. After more than twenty years as an analyst, first for the *Today* show and then for CNN and as a talk-show panelist, I have learned that simply appearing on the home screen earns far more credibility with many people than years of reporting and writing for newspapers. That may be my serious work, but who pays attention? If a tree falls in the forest and all that.

For all the power of the medium, it cannot be said that the television news product has improved. The networks seem to have reached the conclusion that their viewers are less interested in politics and thus have reduced their commitment in terms of both reporters on the story and time on the air. Network executives continue to insist that they devote more resources all the time, but none of the Big Three has a reporter doing basic reporting all through the election cycles as, for example, Ken Bode did for NBC.

The shrinking-sound-bite cliché is accurate. The Center for Media and Public Affairs found that the three major networks' evening news programs devoted 28 percent less time to coverage of the 2000 campaign than they had to the 1988 campaign, the last previous year in which no incumbent president was seeking reelection. With less airtime being used, the candidates' own presence also dwindled predictably—the average sound bite reached a new low of 7.8 seconds.

It is true, of course, that the networks provide institutional coverage with more than ample firepower. Their viewers can expect to be told the top of the news from reporters stationed routinely at the White House, the Pentagon, the State and Justice departments, and both the Senate and House of Representatives. They have reporters who are expert at mining congressional committees for tips on wastes of the taxpayers' money and other skullduggery.

But their coverage of campaigning is largely limited to what is called "the political season"—the period when there are candidates out in the field seeking support. What you don't see very often is network reporters covering meetings of, say, the U.S. Conference of Mayors or the Western Governors' Conference, where the stories are not front-page level.

They also provide those Sunday interview programs—*Meet the Press* on NBC, *Face the Nation* on CBS, and ABC's *This Week* with whomever they trot out to try to compete with Tim Russert. But these programs are largely of interest to the political audience in the capital and a few junkies scattered across the country. The total audience for them is about ten million, which is impressive measured against the circulation of the three or four best newspapers in the country but still far below the levels the networks can command for some of its entertainment programming.

The relatively small audiences perhaps reflect good sense among the potential viewers and potential voters. The goal in these shows is to ask the kind of questions that can produce a story for the Monday-morning newspapers when the person being interviewed either reveals something or, very occasionally, misspeaks. Further, the goal is a story that mentions that this great disclosure was made on their program.

That is not necessarily the same thing, however, as either the interviewer or the viewer learning something that is either new, significant, or interesting, which is one of the definitions of news. The problem with these televised interviews is that the politicians of the stature invited to appear on, let's say, *Meet the Press* are sophisticated enough to decide in advance what they will say when they are asked questions they know are coming and thus are as surprising as a sunset to the politically knowledgeable.

I wouldn't suggest the programs are worthless. Over the years, I have been pleased to appear dozens of times on *Meet the Press* and occasionally on *Face the Nation*. And sometimes we found out something interesting or, at the least, revealed some side of a political figure that had not been previously shown to a national audience. If people didn't know Hubert H. Humphrey was terminally garrulous, they found out one Sunday when he was so long-winded on *Meet the Press,* he only answered five or six questions in the entire half hour. Jack Kemp had a similar problem laid bare on the same show.

There were times, too, when questions had unexpected results. On CBS one Sunday we asked Lloyd Bentsen, running for the Democratic presidential nomination, what kind of car he owned. Bentsen hemmed and hawed a bit, mentioning a pickup truck and a station wagon built in the United States and presumably acceptable to the

United Auto Workers. But eventually he conceded there was a Mercedes in the family. Within a minute after we went off the air, I received a telephone call in the studio from B. A. Bentsen, the senator's wife, who scolded me only half in jest: "Jack Germond, I want you to know you just cost me my Mercedes and I won't forget it."

There are limitations on how much that qualifies as "news" can be gleaned from televised interviews as opposed to quiet one-on-one conversations. And in any case, networks are at the mercy of the powerful to some extent because of their need to "get" the right people. Thus, a White House embattled by some controversy can arrange to put its apologists on all of the Big Three plus Fox and CNN to deliver messages that are remarkably similar and obviously rehearsed.

The primacy of Tim Russert was illustrated most graphically when President George W. Bush chose to appear for the full hour in February 2004 in an attempt to reverse approval ratings that were plunging as more and more potential voters got wise to him. It was also a gesture designed to reassure the Republican troops by showing their leader willing to face the formidable Russert. As it turned out, the interview was taped in the Oval Office and Russert was a pussycat. Bush was rigidly "on message" throughout the hour, making me wonder where I ever got the idea he was wrong to throw out two hundred years of precedent and principle to attack Iraq.

The coverage of politics on cable channels is a puzzle. One of the contradictions is the attention these channels earn from the political players when their audience is so small in comparison with the broadcast networks. The intensity of that audience—the junkie quotient, perhaps—is something the political strategists seemed to recognize long before those of us in the newspaper trade caught wise. The audience for CNN or Fox or MSNBC may be small, but it consists of people who are really interested.

What we also have learned is that there are huge numbers of Americans who watch television all the time without any apparent discrimination or selectivity. I learned that first as a panelist on *The McLaughlin Group* in the early 1980s. Although the show then aired in New York at 8:00 A.M. Saturdays on a public broadcasting outlet, I was frequently recognized on the streets of Manhattan. I was always flattered but puz-zled by this. Who in the world gets up early on a Saturday morning to listen to a bunch of gasbags talking about the latest White House folly?

The breadth of the national audience continued to amaze me. I was stunned, for example, when a young man parking my rental car at a garage in New Orleans started talking about the show and the issues we had been discussing. He even knew that I was a liberal and could repeat back to me the positions I had taken on the topics the previous weekend. I thanked him for his interest, while saying to myself, Get a life, young man, get a life.

On another occasion I spent three months as a temporary fill-in an-chor on a cable channel long since deceased called America's Talking. It was run by Roger Ailes, the erstwhile Republican hired gun and media expert later to be the prime mover in the success of the Fox News Channel. It was based at an NBC satellite operation in Fort Lee, New Jersey, and its prime news program aired five nights a week from 6:00 to 8:00 P.M. with one anchor at Fort Lee and the other in Wash-ington.

Ailes paid me handsomely to keep the Washington seat warm for a permanent replacement who was obliged to remain in Los Angeles for a while. I showed up at around five after my day job writing for the Baltimore *Sun* and was handed a folder of clippings on the day's news to read while I was getting made up to go on the air an hour later. The format was a series of live interviews with putative experts on whatever story we were doing, plus taking telephone calls from viewers. Amer-ica's Talking, get it?

As it happened, this stint came during the O. J. Simpson trial, and every evening we had two or three panels of criminal lawyers and for-mer federal prosecutors—isn't every lawyer a former federal prosecu-tor?—as well as a handful of guests on other topics as diverse as defense policy, crime, and abortion rights. Guests were not hard to find even for this outlet. One of the facts of media life is that everyone wants to be on television.

I found doing two hours of live television an exhausting tour de force, and I fled the studio every night to dive into a martini and a steak as quickly as possible. I also learned that even this obscure channel had a large enough audience that I could expect viewers to accost me in airports. They had to be people, I concluded, who watched everything from wrestling to *Masterpiece Theater.*

That instant celebrity is, of course, beguiling. As someone said long ago, the trick is not to inhale. The trick also is to understand that being on television, where they like to talk about themselves as "journalists," doesn't make you a reporter. The real business of network television is entertainment, not news. Even big stories can't match *The Simpsons.*

7

THOSE INSIDIOUS POLLS

*E*arly in 1998 Republicans from thirteen southern states gathered on the Gulf Coast at Biloxi, Mississippi, to play the slot machines, listen to the country singers who were not quite big enough for Las Vegas or Branson, and take a reading on the party's potential presidential nominees in 2000.

The Republicans were feeling pretty giddy, and with good reason. The party had control of both houses of Congress, and there were indications the GOP could gain a few more seats in the South in the coming election. The prospect of succeeding President Bill Clinton was heady—and they didn't yet know the full tawdry story of the president of the United States playing slap-and-tickle with some chubby White House intern. The early field of Republican candidates, most of whom were to speak at the conference, included some of the usual suspects—former Vice President Dan Quayle, Jack Kemp, Steve Forbes, Lamar Alexander—and some different if not necessarily fresh faces— among them John Ashcroft, John Kasich, and Elizabeth Dole.

But the Big Enchilada in the Republican hierarchy was Governor George W. Bush of Texas, who was so far ahead of the pack he could afford to give the event in Biloxi a pass. His lead in the opinion polls was so clearly beyond the reach of his competitors that Republicans from all elements of the party were arriving in Austin almost weekly to pledge their support and, more to the point, press money on his campaign. It wasn't even close. It was time to get on board or miss the express.

The delegates at Biloxi reflected Bush's primacy. He was their choice because the polls said so. Asked what they liked about Bush, these southern Republican activists all seemed to get back to those magic poll numbers. He was defeating all the other Republicans easily for the nomination and running even with or ahead of Vice President Al Gore, the leading contender for the Democratic nomination. What else do you need to know?

The whole thing was, nonetheless, an illusion. Most of the respondents to the polls didn't know anything about George W. Bush other than that he was governor of Texas, and many of the delegates at Biloxi seemed a little vague on that. No one could tell me anything he had accomplished at the state level or anything specific that they liked about him. In national surveys, pollsters thought at least a significant minority of respondents believed the questions were referring to his father, George H. W. Bush.

But in the strange world of politics today, the fact that George W. Bush's recognition factor was built on little information or misinformation didn't really matter. Being "ahead in the polls" was the most important credential, no matter how it was achieved. Even hardheaded political professionals find it difficult to put those numbers in perspective.

It is tempting to infer from this history that the whole Bush presidency was an accidental product of the opinion polls. That would absolve the electorate, perhaps. But although not totally outlandish, that notion is a bit of a stretch. Bush had shown he could be an attractive candidate by winning in Texas, and he benefited from the machinations of Karl Rove, an Austin consultant of demonstrated skills, and a highly professional campaign apparatus. However, the polling data, flawed though it may have been, was significant in moving Bush to the front of the pack by bringing so much of the Republican power structure and so much money behind his candidacy. By the time the primaries began, many Republicans had an enormous investment of one kind or another in his success.

The opinion surveys were not enough to clear his path. When Bush was revealed to New Hampshire voters as something other than a name, the emptiness of those poll numbers and the emptiness of the candidate became clear to everyone paying attention. Over roughly eight months voters in that primary were able to compare the real George W. Bush with another Republican who became equally known to them, Senator John McCain of Arizona. And Bush's loss to McCain in a landslide, by 18 percent, was a harsh verdict indeed. It seemed those early polls were irrelevant when real decisions had to be made—except, of course, for the cushion in money and backing they provided in the first place.

Bush used that cushion to save his candidacy. He responded to misfortune in New Hampshire with a well-financed comeback campaign that displayed his personal tenacity and his willingness to use venal negative attacks to scuttle McCain. The centerpiece of his political resuscitation was, of course, the Big Lie—his campaign to present himself as "A Reformer with Results," the implication being that he was not just a self-proclaimed reformer like that damned McCain.

Like his father before him, Bush proved to be one of those candidates from the upper reaches of polite society who are not averse to playing the rawest kind of negative politics—so long as it is done by the hired guns and doesn't require getting your own hands dirty. Before it was over, the Bush campaign depicted Vietnam War hero McCain as, among other things, a member of Congress who was inattentive to the concerns of veterans and indifferent to victims of breast cancer, a group, incidentally, that included McCain's own sister.

The Arizona senator made some political mistakes and suffered from a shortage of money after New Hampshire. But the critical factor in his inability to compete effectively was that there were no more occasions in the campaign schedule on which he could force the voters to take a close look at both candidates over an extended period. So, although Bush wasn't just a creature of opinion polls warped by igno-rance in the electorate, his road to the White House began as a case of mistaken identity.

This is the single most damning complaint against the opinion polls that have become such a force in American politics. Understandably, the pollsters don't want to advertise the questions about their role in public affairs. But there are problems. Some are relatively minor, sim-ply a function of changes in our technology. It is harder for the poll takers to construct a reliable sample with so many cell phones in use and a highly mobile population of potential respondents. Americans annoyed by telemarketing also are refusing to submit to questioning in increasing numbers, to the point that poll takers sometimes must make several times the number of calls needed to provide an adequate sample.

The real problem, however, is something frankly impossible to cor-rect. It is ignorance, pure and simple. Many of those who answer the questions don't know what they are talking about. Some of them don't want to appear as uninformed as they are, so they answer the questions with a stab in the dark. Or they allow themselves to be pressed into doing so by the pollster. Some just don't know how little they know. And some simply want to be helpful and cooperative with this nice person on the telephone who seems to care what they think. The re-sult is that the polls are often only reflections of name recognition, as in the case of mistaking one George Bush for another.

There is nothing new about such ignorance. As a student at the University of Missouri in 1950, I took a job with the R. L. Polk Com-pany, publishers of city directories, canvassing parts of Boonville, Mis-souri, the home state of then President Harry S Truman. The survey included a few public-affairs questions along with those seeking opin-ions on brands of tooth powder and shampoo. I was shocked to find that well over half the people I questioned in a middle-class neighbor-hood could not identify Alben Barkley, who was vice president of the United States.

Sometimes the voters' ignorance can lead to laughable errors. In the 1968 Democratic primary in New Hampshire, for instance, Senator Eugene J. McCarthy of Minnesota won a de facto triumph by polling 42 percent against a sitting president, Lyndon B. Johnson, in what was considered evidence of growing popular disenchantment with the Johnson policy in promulgating the Vietnam War. That inference was legitimate enough, but students of the primary found after the fact that some of those dissident voters thought they were supporting not the liberal from Minnesota but instead the late Senator Joe McCarthy of Wisconsin, the notorious hunter of Communists in government fifteen years earlier.

The message then—and now—is that fewer people are paying attention than the politicians imagine. And their indifference can have consequences.

The hazard in the reliance on the polls has more to do with issues than with people. A politician can overcome a lack of name recognition simply by being on the television screens every night, either in news coverage or advertising. Many Americans refuse to pay attention even then, but some information seems to leak through the blood-brain barrier, like it or not, so that after a time they can identify people who were just a face on the television screens a few weeks or months earlier. And the polls can accurately forecast election results to the extent that voters cast their ballots on the basis of the same ignorance and name recognition that they display in the surveys.

But we are venturing into far more sensitive territory when we use polls to measure the popular will on anything but the simplest propositions. If we ask voters how they stand on a proposed SALT III disarmament treaty, we are inviting misleading results. How many people know enough about disarmament to have an informed opinion? Isn't that why we elect people whose judgment we trust? Isn't the expectation that, once elected, they will in turn hire disarmament officials whose expertise they trust? Indeed, any elected official who fails to make such appointments should be defeated. And so should anyone who takes advice on complex issues from opinion polls. It is not a question of the polls being "wrong" but instead of their being meaningless.

The true menace here is that too often the politician—president or otherwise—will yield to the tyranny of the majority and allow himself to base votes and policies on the poll numbers or even on the mail count from constituents. It happens all the time, although neither the officeholders nor their staff members like to admit it. The situation can be tricky when, for example, a politician is accosted by someone from CNN asking, "The polls show seventy-one percent of the people say we should stay in Iraq at least six more months; what do you say to that?"

The truthful answer might be "They don't know what they're talking about, but I know the facts and I'm going to vote my conscience." Instead, the politician must waffle about how complex the problem seems to be, and so on and so forth, but don't forget I'm supporting the troops of course. Who wants to risk defying the polls? That might even be seen as providing leadership.

In his often-cited speech to the electors of Bristol in the eighteenth century, Edmund Burke defined the politician's responsibility this way: "Your representative owes you, not his industry only, but his judgment, and he betrays, instead of serving you, if he sacrifices it to your opinion." It is probably safe to say there are not many Edmund Burkes in Congress or the White House, just as there were no polls in 1774 and no approval ratings for Edmund Burke to consider.

Those approval ratings are based on the same limited knowledge or, again, plain ignorance as the answers to other questions. And to the degree that they are based on such a flimsy foundation, they are often subject to quick change. That is why so many campaign strategists are so frantic about finding the magic hit on the networks that may change a perception of their candidate overnight.

The surveys can be most valuable when they are used to follow trends, usually by repeating the same questions in one survey after another so that changes are uncovered and quantified. The favorite guide of many political professionals is a question most pollsters have been asking for years as to whether the country—or the state or city—is "headed in the right direction" or "off on the wrong track." If the "wrong track" number rises past 50 percent, it is a warning to incumbent politicians that they may be in jeopardy. If it goes past 60 or 70 percent, the politician should find other work.

Given those rules of thumb, I was surprised when the 1992 campaign to reelect the first President Bush ignored a "wrong track" that went from below 20 percent after the Persian Gulf War to the 60 to 70 percent range by the time the campaign began in earnest a year later. It was a classic case of hubris. How could the man who won the war lose the election so soon thereafter? It just wasn't fair. This had to be the exception to the rule.

Certainly no presidential campaign can claim a lack of information. The amount spent on polls by campaigns and political organizations is probably far greater than the outlays on the so-called "public" polls, meaning the Gallup Poll, for example. All campaigns of even modest pretensions hire pollsters. So does the White House, whether Republican or Democratic, often for daily surveys paid for by the Republican and Democratic National Committees and fed into the offices of the president's political advisers. They seem to think it is essential to take the national temperature every day even if they know all the flaws in the polls. How would a president know which way to lead the nation if he didn't know which way the people wanted to go? And presidents usually want to know. At least two in my memory, Lyndon Johnson and Richard Nixon, were known to carry the latest survey results in their inside jacket pocket, available to consult or display at a moment's notice.

The truth, often overlooked, is that all big-league politicians are working from essentially the same data. Reputable pollsters use methods refined over the years to achieve a remarkable accuracy, so Republicans and Democrats operate from the same base of knowledge. This often pushes them all toward the safe middle of the road. It is no accident that so many Democrats now support the death penalty and so many Republicans more federal spending on education.

Polls are also important for raising money for candidates and for deciding which candidates should benefit from the contributors' largesse—no point in wasting dollars on hopeless cases, after all. So each of the parties' organizations committed to electing right-thinking people to the Senate and House of Representatives poll extensively. And many candidates for local offices with more money than good sense commission polls when fewer than 10 percent of their constituents have even a foggy idea about their campaigns.

It is no surprise that the polls are often manipulated by campaign operatives with varying degrees of sophistication. At the most elementary level, campaign strategists working in New Hampshire, for example, make a point of knowing when *The Boston Globe* has a poll in the field and the dates on which the interviewing will be done. That's when they suddenly make a big television-advertising buy to expose their candidate's name and face to those who might be polled. The result is almost always a misleading gain in the candidate's poll position, which can then be used to raise more money for more TV spots the next time the *Globe* pollster is in the field. Sooner or later, your candidate may become the one "leading in all the polls," which is practically the same thing as being elected.

Campaign operatives will also leak poll results to reporters, particularly those who will report them uncritically, in the hope of building at least the appearance of political momentum. There are so many organizations purporting to report "news" these days that there is always someone to rush the fresh figures into the public domain. By the standards of much of what passes for journalism on the home screen, that is considered a scoop.

The role of the poll takers within campaigns varies widely, perhaps with the inclination of the candidate to rely on survey research. In many presidential campaigns they become part of the inner circle of strategic advisers whose knowledge of the electorate is presumed to be special. Patrick Caddell, for example, polled for Jimmy Carter and continued as part of his team of political advisers inside the White House. Robert Teeter, a Republican of platinum credentials and long experience, was a key man in the elder George Bush's campaign-management team.

Often the most valuable service pollsters can provide to a candidate is giving the campaign insight into what may be fertile ground. The poll takers frequently use "focus groups," meaning eight or ten or twelve people brought together to offer their responses in discussions led by the campaign professionals. When Walter Mondale's 1984 campaign for the Democratic nomination seemed in jeopardy, a focus group put together by Peter Hart showed the way out.

When they were asked who would be better on a range of economic and domestic issues, the members of the group were strongly for Gary Hart as the "fresh face" bringing "new ideas." But when asked who they would trust most in an international confrontation, the hands all shot up for Mondale. And that reaction gave birth to what became known somewhat famously in political circles as "the red telephone ad"—a television commercial showing a loudly ringing red telephone, obviously suggesting a direct line either to Moscow or the Strategic Air Command. The viewer was expected to infer that the ringing of that particular telephone indicated a dire international crisis probably involving the threat of nuclear war. The spot was widely credited with at least temporarily slowing Hart's momentum.

A few pollsters simply provide the survey data and then walk away, leaving it to the campaign flacks to try to present the data in a positive light. They are sometimes fired if their findings don't please the candidate who is paying their fees, although that might seem to defeat the purpose of survey research in the first place. In Little Rock ten days before the 1980 election Governor Bill Clinton of Arkansas told me two things—that he was well on his way to reelection to a second term and, incidentally, that he had replaced his pollster because he was being given "bad numbers" he could not trust. Ten days later Clinton was defeated by Frank White, a Republican and avant-garde fundamentalist who believed creationism should be taught in the public schools. So much for bad numbers.

The neatest trick performed by some pollsters is their ability to tell their candidate one thing, potential campaign contributors quite another, and reporters still another without losing credibility with any of these numbers consumers. The explanation is that the pollster produces several different sets of figures that are predicated on different statistical models of the turnout. That optimistic report given the press may be based on a totally unlikely premise of a stampede to the polling places. But reporters who have been around the track understand where the poll takers' first loyalty must lie and how that colors what they can say.

Sorting out the pollsters is much more difficult these days than it was two generations ago, when there were only a half dozen who worked for candidates and only three public polls of national prominence—those run by George Gallup, Louis Harris, and Elmo Roper. A measure of how small the political universe was in those days could be taken in 1967, when Gallup decided that national political reporters needed to know more about how surveys were conducted so they could ask better questions and report more accurately.

He invited all those reporters who covered national politics full-time—only about a dozen of us in that era—to a two-day seminar at his headquarters in Princeton, New Jersey. Several of us suspected Gallup's initiative was a kind of left-handed comment on his prime rival, Harris, who had close connections to the Kennedy campaign in 1960 and the Democratic administration. Harris apparently shared that suspicion and invited the same reporters to a daylong tutorial at the National Press Club in Washington a month or so after the seminar in Princeton.

In both cases the pollsters explained in detail how questions were written, samples derived, interviews conducted, and statistical method applied. The theory was that if we were properly instructed, we would recognize a legitimate poll and understand what weight to give it. And that, in turn, would make our stories more accurate reflections of the facts and less susceptible to exaggerated claims for the latest survey research.

These days such a notion seems hopelessly quaint. There are so many polls being conducted by so many people, the chances of sorting the wheat from the chaff are slim under the best circumstances. Even some ostensibly legitimate surveys are doing ridiculous things in the obvious interest of making a profit from gullible local television stations and, I am sorry to add, newspapers. Thus, we have one poll claiming to cover the South with a sample of twelve hundred, a reasonable number, but then offering results from Tennessee or Alabama when the sample for each state cannot be more than one hundred respondents. These are pollsters who will tell you what African Americans are thinking based on a sample of twenty-eight.

Some are notorious among the political professionals who suspect they may not even be doing the interviews because their results always reflect the biases of their clients. Others skew the wording of questions to elicit the desired response. In a report on polling in 2003, the Brookings Institution cited one beauty from a survey made for the Augusta National Golf Club, site of the Masters tournament, when it was besieged by Martha Burk and the National Council of Women's Organizations seeking admission of women as members of the club. Respondents were asked to agree or disagree with these two statements:

- Martha Burk did not really care if the Augusta National Golf Club began allowing women members, she was more concerned with attracting media attention for herself and her organization.
- In a way, Ms. Burk's actions are insulting to women because it makes it seem that getting admitted to a golf club is a big priority to all women.

Guess how that one turned out?

The sponsorship of polls by the press also raises some serious questions. It must be conceded at the outset that political reporters rely heavily on the survey data to tell them where a campaign stands. Any political reporter who doesn't answer the readers' first question—who's winning?—will soon be covering Rotary Club luncheons or the board of education. And at the most sophisticated level of both politics and journalism, it is possible to make good guesses from the polls being taken about where a campaign is strong or weak and on which issues. Weighed with a proper skepticism, they provide better guidance than the county chairman or ward leader on whom we might have relied in another time.

The real sin of the press on polling is the insistence on every self-respecting news organization having its own poll or sharing the proprietorship with some other heavyweight operation. If we have CBS News–*New York Times*, it follows that we must have ABC News–*Washington Post*, NBC–*Wall Street Journal*, and CNN-*Time*-Gallup. We are, in short, overwhelmed with polls duplicating one another in quantifying the obvious.

Nor are the big national polls the only ones. There are statewide surveys of some standing in, among other states, California, Oregon, Iowa, Illinois, Massachusetts, Minnesota, Maryland, New Hampshire, New York, Pennsylvania, and Florida. And there are dozens of other polls produced for cabals of small television stations, not always with strict attention to the niceties of the Gallup method. Many of them are a bad joke.

But as empty and boring as they may be, editors seem to love them. When *Time* magazine bought the *Washington Star* shortly before the 1980 presidential campaign, I proposed in my lofty capacity as senior political reporter that rather than running a lot of dull stories that would say the same thing as everyone else's dull stories, we should treat the polls like the baseball statistics summarized on every sports page. We would run the latest results in a table of small type that would show the date of the survey, the size of the sample, and the figures. Then if something newsworthy happened, we would carry a separate story just as the sports pages would supplement the agate type and publish stories on, let's say, a hitter batting .400 in July.

I thought it was a dandy idea, but the editor from *Time,* presiding over the declining days of the *Star,* decided instead to assign one of our best reporters to write about nothing but polls, which she did ad nauseam throughout the campaign. So much for my clout.

The fundamental problem with news organizations getting into the polling business is the way it may shape their coverage of the campaign. If your newspaper has taken a poll and found Al Gore trailing on Monday, there is a temptation to allow that data to find its way into your story Tuesday. Gore is now not just "the Democratic candidate" but the "hard-pressed Democratic candidate" who is "bringing his troubled campaign into Philadelphia." In fact, as a reporter, you may not know why he is campaigning in Pennsylvania and it may have nothing to do with his standing in the polls and everything to do with some particular group he needs to reach or perhaps with a promise made to the mayor of Philadelphia in exchange for his endorsement five months ago.

The most indefensible use of proprietary polling data by a news organization in my time was a story perpetrated by ABC News on its main evening program, *World News Tonight,* the night before the second and final debate of the 1988 campaign.

The story (if that is what it was) took up more than twelve minutes of the half-hour show, and it dealt such an unfair blow to the Dukakis campaign that even Republican professionals in the Bush campaign admitted feeling sympathy for their hapless foe. It was introduced by anchorman Peter Jennings in extravagant terms as "something that has not been done before" and as "the most comprehensive poll of the entire campaign for the White House." The survey "just conducted," Jennings pronounced, had covered "each of the fifty states" and a sample of almost ten thousand likely voters and had found George H. W. Bush the "overwhelming favorite" to win the election.

Jennings's assurances were based on sand. For one thing, some of the polling included was three weeks old, which in a presidential campaign hardly qualifies as "just conducted." More to the point, the ludicrous suggestion that the poll could tell what was happening in "each of the fifty states" was laughable to anyone knowledgeable about polls although not to the poor suckers watching the program and putting their trust in Jennings. Ten thousand interviews spread over fifty states comes to two hundred per state, a sample so small that in some states the margin of error might be plus or minus 10 percent. If you took Jennings's account at face value, and there would be no reason for most viewers not to do so, the campaign was essentially all over. Bush held a firm lead in so many states that Dukakis would need a miracle to overtake him. In fact, the popular-vote margin in the ABC News–*Washington Post* national poll showed the Bush lead at 51 percent to 46 percent, not an irreversible margin at that stage of the campaign.

But ABC News had decided to seize the ultimate advantage over its competitors and declare the election over three weeks ahead of time.

How's that for great reporting? Take that, Brokaw. Eat your heart out, Rather.

Good political stories cannot ignore the relative position of a candidate, but as ABC News demonstrated, getting into the polling business adds an element to the equation that probably shouldn't be there. Besides, why do you need still another survey of the same old stuff? Most of your readers and viewers don't give a damn anyway.

8

LYING ABOUT RACE

*N*obody in politics or the press tells the truth about race. The politicians talk about it and around it, and the reporters write about it and around it. But neither is candid in dealing with what is the single most influential factor in American politics today. We don't talk about how the Democrats rely on the blacks and are fettered by that reliance. We don't talk about how the Republicans play to the racial resentments of whites and are tarnished by that tactic.

The evidence is abundant. You can make a convincing argument that candidate Bill Clinton won the presidency in 1992 by instigating the Sister Souljah episode. At the same time, he demonstrated how pivotal race continues to be in American politics long after the Voting Rights Act of 1965 unleashed the black vote.

Once elected, President Clinton denied that the incident was prompted by a hope for political gain. Appropriately enough, that denial demonstrated how difficult it is in politics to tell the truth about race. It rarely happens. Pandering is one thing, admitting to it quite another.

At the most elementary level, Clinton was motivated by the need to solve the "problem" of Jesse Jackson, who once again was seeking the special attention he had demanded of two previous Democratic nominees for president, Walter F. Mondale in 1984 and Michael S. Dukakis in 1988. This time Jackson was not competing for attention as a candidate himself; he was demanding recognition as the prime spokesman for African Americans.

And with the Democratic National Convention approaching in July, he was not discouraging calls from his admirers for Clinton to choose him to be the vice presidential nominee, something Mondale and Dukakis had fended off awkwardly and belatedly in those earlier campaigns. Telling Jackson that the country wouldn't accept him or any other black candidate was not an easy sell. Both Mondale and Dukakis recognized the risks.

Clinton, just as adamantly opposed to the notion of Jackson on the ticket, understood the situation fully. He was feeling pressure from political allies, particularly in the South, to—as one major contributor from Alabama told me at the time—"tell old Jesse where to stuff it." He needed not only to stymie any movement for Jackson but to do it in a way that was clear to anyone paying attention to the campaign and still be acceptable to the many prominent black leaders already behind his candidacy.

As it happened, just such an opportunity presented itself that June as the de facto presidential nominee was on the way to a meeting in Washington of Jackson's Rainbow Coalition. Clinton's unintentional benefactor was a woman named Lisa Williamson, a rap singer who performed under the name Sister Souljah.

A month earlier *The Washington Post* had published an interview with the entertainer in which she was asked if the violence carried out by blacks in the Los Angeles riots was "wise." To which she replied: "Yeah, it was wise. I mean if black people kill black people every day, why not have a week and kill white people? . . . In other words, white people, this government and the mayor were well aware of the fact that black people were dying every day in Los Angeles under gang violence. So if you're a gang member and you normally would be killing somebody, why not kill a white person?"

It was, of course, outlandish, and Sister Souljah's stupidity was matched only by that of the reporter or editor at the *Post* who decided there would be news value in the opinion of a rap singer on the Los Angeles violence. It's a wonder they didn't take a poll of the whole entertainment community and give us the verdict in percentages.

Clinton, flying into Washington, was gratified to discover that Sister Souljah had spoken to Jackson's Rainbow Coalition just one day before he was to address the same group. He had always been a politician who seized and exploited targets of opportunity. So, with Jackson seated next to him on the podium, he chastised the organization for providing a public forum for the rap singer. Her remarks about Los Angeles, said Clinton, were "filled with a kind of hatred that you do not honor today and tonight." Then he added, "If you took the words *white* and *black* and reversed them, you might think David Duke [a notorious white racist politician in Louisiana] was giving that speech."

Jackson, who could find an insult behind any tree if it suited him, was predictably outraged. And his mood wasn't lightened by Clinton telling him in a private meeting shortly after his speech that he would not be chosen for the vice presidential nomination. When Clinton told him his campaign had polling numbers that showed Jackson wouldn't be a good fit, Jackson replied that he had his own numbers that would show how much he could bring to the ticket. Both of them were obviously humming a few bars and making it up as they went along, but the message was clear. Clinton was choosing someone else, and Jackson was not going quietly into the night. Big surprise.

For candidate Clinton, though, the significant thing was that the story of him affronting Jackson on Sister Souljah was given instant and widespread attention. He had not only affronted him, but he had done it at a meeting of "the Rainbow," as the civil rights leader always referred to his organization in reverential tones. So, to no one's surprise, Jackson continued to complain into any live microphone about how shabbily he was being treated by Clinton despite his own restraint on earlier occasions when he might have been angered by the man now dissing him.

The rebuff resounded throughout the campaign from June through October. I heard about it from middle-class white voters in small towns in Alabama and blue-collar suburbs of Philadelphia and gritty urban neighborhoods in northern New Jersey. This guy was something different, just like he claimed. He had the nerve to tell off Jesse Jackson. It's about time. He's not another Mondale or Dukakis.

These were the white voters then called "Reagan Democrats" who made up the prime target for Bill Clinton when he presented himself as "the different kind of Democrat"—meaning one who is not a patsy for liberal causes and minorities like Mondale and Dukakis were. These were the voters who believed that Clinton's promise to "end welfare as we know it" was really code for less welfare for lazy blacks paid for by the taxes of the hardworking whites. In the end these were the voters whose return to the Democratic line, particularly in the industrial states, made the difference in the defeat of incumbent Republican president George H. W. Bush.

The operative dynamic was racism or racial resentment or whatever label you might prefer. Although the national ethic now includes an America free of racism, you cannot transform a society in two or three generations. Most Americans today are too young to have a clear personal memory of how segregation stained the nation and why the civil rights movement was necessary. They may know about Martin Luther King, Jr., only as a martyred figure from the past. But they see Jesse Jackson joining every protest and spewing alliterative anger as a spokesman for black America while the television cameras roll.

Jackson's influence clearly waned in the 1990s because of his unwillingness to run for mayor of the District of Columbia, a reluctance taken as an indicator of a lack of commitment to political action as opposed to protest. But it is also true that Jackson has been the center of black-white politics in America at the national level since 1984, the year he made his first campaign for the Democratic presidential nomination. It was an instructive candidacy for both blacks and whites.

Neither the other Democratic candidates nor the press knew quite how to deal with a black making a serious run for the presidency as opposed to the admittedly symbolic effort by Representative Shirley Chisholm, also a Democrat, in 1972. When Jackson made factual errors on things like the level of defense spending or how the budget process worked, nobody pointed out his mistakes as evidence that he was out of his depth or had not done his homework. For one thing, we all knew that he would never win the nomination and become president, so it didn't matter if he was a little fuzzy on the details. More to the point, if you dwelled on his errors, there was the danger of being accused of racism. Nobody, reporter or politician, wanted that.

Even when Jackson was shown—by a black reporter for *The Washington Post,* incidentally—to have referred to Jews as "Hymies" and to New York as "Hymietown," his rivals for the nomination tried to look the other way. They did the same in being so slow to confront his alliance with the blatantly anti-Semitic Louis Farrakhan and the Nation of Islam. Nobody wanted to alienate any segment of the black electorate, a constituency that gives 85 to 90 percent or more of its vote to any Democratic candidate.

This concern among Democrats was reinforced by the discovery that Jackson had a broader reach in the African-American community than the political experts had forecast when he declared his candidacy. At the outset, he had been seen as a symbolic candidate who would build his following among lower-income unskilled workers and young blacks attracted to his style and personal force rather than among middle-class blacks who apparently had moved beyond protest politics.

That judgment was dead wrong. All over the country his reach along racial lines was broad. In random interviewing among middle-class black voters in two Philadelphia neighborhoods, for example, I found almost universal support for "the reverend," as many called him. It came from, among others, accountants, teachers, letter carriers, business executives, lawyers, public employees, and the proprietors of stores and restaurants.

Some of them found his flamboyant style a little hard to swallow. But they admired the nerve he showed in running, and they took particular pride in the skill he displayed in the televised debates with the white politicians. Jesse Jackson was no second-class citizen on the stump. He could hold his own. If anything, he was a better speaker than anyone in the party with the possible exception of Mario Cuomo.

The only significant reservations in the black community came from several leaders of the civil rights movement—most notably Andrew Young, John Lewis, Julian Bond, Coretta Scott King—who found a comfortable alternative in Mondale. These black leaders remembered Jackson as a young and decidedly minor player in the entourage of Martin Luther King, Jr., and they were convinced he had overstepped propriety and history in the claims he made about his status. Some were particularly offended by his appearance waving a bloody shirt on the NBC *Today* program the morning after King was shot and killed in Memphis in 1968.

Even for whites not weighted down with racism, Jackson was a little imposing. Here was this big, scowling black man, speaking in rhyming couplets and loudly demanding respect for his people. In fact, if anyone stopped to listen, they found the Jackson message was benign. It was delivered largely to young people whom he urged to stay in school, avoid drugs, and take part in politics and public affairs as a way to advance their own lives.

The quality and nature of Jackson's rhetoric never received enough attention from the press or, perhaps as a consequence, from the voters. And Jackson himself was largely to blame. Are the cameras going to parse a speech to show its true nature? Or would they prefer to focus on Jackson, in full alliteration, complaining about the lack of respect he is being given by his rivals? For years Jackson marched to the head of every parade of protesters capable of attracting the cameras. Indeed, his insistence on pushing his way to the front whenever the TV lights went on became a standing joke among politicians, both black and white, who observed him at close range.

In the end, the mistaken perception of Mondale's efforts to placate Jackson created many of those Reagan Democrats. In Alabama, high school girls returned to Mondale campaign headquarters in tears after passing out Mondale literature at traffic lights and being called "nigger lovers." In most southern states the national Democratic campaign was stifled in its cradle.

The former vice president had locked up the nomination for all practical purposes in early June, when he won the New Jersey primary and enough delegates in California to claim a majority at the impending convention in San Francisco. (In fact, Mondale's lead over his prime challenger, Gary Hart, was only a few more than a hundred delegates, but only one or two advisers to Mondale were fully aware of how thin the ice really was.) Yet even after Mondale was nominated by the convention, Jackson would not endorse him—at least not in so many words. And his refusal to do so, Jackson was fully aware, made a story the press pursued relentlessly. Reporters picked at it for weeks while Jackson complained that he and his constituency were not being given the "respect" to which they were entitled.

Just why the use of the word *endorse* was so important isn't easy to explain to ordinary voters who are logical people not inclined to vote on the basis of someone else's recommendation. The reporters, myself included, considered it a story because the usual thing to do in politics was to swallow a defeat and go along. The losing candidate who refused to make that gesture in an intraparty situation would be suspected of harboring dark reservations and trying to discourage his erstwhile followers.

In Jackson's case, the value of an endorsement was suggested by the higher black turnout he attracted in the primaries where he was on the ballot. It was important enough that the Mondale campaign went to great lengths to enlist other black leaders to appeal to Jackson.

Mondale and his managers didn't know how to deal with Jackson, and they had been fretting about it for months. Sharing a beer and some cheese with Mondale late one night during the New Hampshire primary, I asked him how he was going to handle Jackson. Mondale laughed, puffed on his cigar, and replied: "Verrry carefully."

It never worked. The first responsibility for dealing with the prickly civil rights leader was given to Bob Beckel, a crafty and seasoned professional in one of the campaign's top jobs. He was convinced he could establish a rapport with Jackson eventually, but Jackson derided the Mondale advisers behind their backs and continued to press his demands for a larger part in the campaign and the Democratic Party.

Indeed, he stirred up his followers to the point that during the San Francisco convention they booed Andrew Young, one of the two or three people closest to Martin Luther King and a man who had endured years of sacrifice and abuse so the people doing the booing could even be in the hall. And when Coretta Scott King interceded and scolded the booing delegates, many of them hooted at her as well. What have they done for us lately? Andy Young and the widow of Martin Luther King were old news.

Even after the convention, Jackson continued to go his own way until the Labor Day weekend was looming without an endorsement. The Mondale campaign convened a meeting in St. Paul of several dozen black political leaders from all over the country, including those who had supported Jackson as well as Mondale in the primaries. The idea was to send a message of united support that black voters could not mistake.

Jackson required special handling, of course. A private meeting beforehand with the candidate was arranged at the Mondales' home outside the Twin Cities, and Jackson showed up two hours late. And then there was to be a joint press conference in an elementary school yard. All of the reporters covering the meeting expected that long-delayed endorsement. It was Saturday night of Labor Day weekend, not a great time to win a huge audience for the news but better than nothing.

Predictably, it didn't happen. Mondale stood there, a fixed smile on his face, digging his wing-tipped toe into the gravel while Jackson humiliated him by refusing to use the word *endorse*. I recall feeling an unprofessional sympathy for Fritz Mondale. The word didn't mean much, and what the hell, Mondale was going to be buried by Reagan anyway. He didn't need this crap.

There are, nonetheless, standards of behavior in politics that Jesse Jackson clearly felt entitled to ignore. His concern was "the community" rather than the Democratic Party and its national ticket and their chance of replacing an administration black Americans overwhelmingly considered hostile.

Asked repeatedly whether he was "endorsing" Mondale at long last, Jackson indulged himself with one circumlocution after another: "We have embraced the mission and support the Mondale-Ferraro ticket with great fervor. My support will be wide-based, deep, and intense." Or: "We will campaign together and present the solid front we need for victory."

The word *endorse* never passed his lips. And Mondale and his advisers were furious as they drove downtown to the St. Paul Hotel to meet with the other black leaders. They knew what the story would be. They never confronted Jackson, something Mondale probably should have done right after the convention if not earlier. The message should have been "Get on board before it's too late." What the hell, where else was Jackson going to go?

In the end, after a long and contentious meeting with the candidate, the black leaders gathered at the St. Paul Hotel finally delivered an endorsement that Jesse Jackson was forced to join. Coleman Young, the mayor of Detroit, who had never disguised his dislike for Jackson, made no bones about the pleasure he took in affixing a big MONDALE-FERRARO sticker to Jackson's lapel while the television cameras rolled. Long after the fact, Jackson conceded, "I finally concluded that we had more at stake than just Fritz."

The whole thing came too late, however, and the impression that Mondale had caved in to Jesse Jackson to get black support added measurably to the number of Reagan Democrats in the November electorate.

Four years later another liberal Democrat, Michael S. Dukakis, went through something similar—winning a presidential nomination while allowing himself to be seen as being jerked around by Jesse Jackson.

The Massachusetts governor was dogged by Jackson through the primaries, the civil rights leader carrying his losing but noisy campaign right through the California primary the first week in June. Once the nomination was settled, he began campaigning to be the choice for vice president. He had finished second in the primaries, he argued, and he had been given seven million votes, so now he should be on the national ticket.

There was, of course, no such tradition or even habit in the Democratic Party. John F. Kennedy had chosen Lyndon B. Johnson in 1960 in the hopes of strengthening his hand in the South. But Jimmy Carter had been under no pressure to choose Morris Udall, his closest pursuer, in 1976, nor Mondale to choose Gary Hart in 1984. But Jackson's argument was advanced with enough vehemence that Dukakis was clearly not free to choose one of the other also-rans of 1988, such as then House Majority Leader Richard Gephardt or Senator Al Gore. That would have produced howls of outrage from Jackson arguing that he had been passed over because he was black.

It would have been true, of course, but in dealing with race questions, there is little premium on truth telling. The risk of a breach with the black community was simply too great.

So the Dukakis campaign tiptoed around Jackson, trying to placate him with one special gesture after another, none of them lost on the conservative white Democrats who had deserted Mondale in 1984 and were quite ready to do it again for, of all people, the preppy Republican George Herbert Walker Bush.

Jackson took advantage of the special insulation afforded him by his race and continued to agitate publicly for the vice presidency, sometimes urging only that he be considered, other times indicating that choosing anyone else would amount to a rejection on racial grounds. The Dukakis campaign was trapped when the candidate invited Jackson and his wife to join them in their home in Boston for a family dinner on July 4, to be followed by viewing the fireworks from the banks of the Charles River. If that wasn't a signal of proper respect to a fellow Democrat, what in the world would qualify?

The evening was a mixed success. The dinner was traditional New England fare for the holiday—New England clam chowder, poached salmon in a cream sauce, an ice cream sundae. But Jackson was lactose-intolerant, which his staff had failed to pass on to the Dukakis campaign, so the chowder, sauce, and ice cream were a problem. Later in the evening, the hungry Jackson, not overly concerned about the sensibilities of his hosts, sent one of his staff for fried chicken he could eat on the banks of the Charles.

Despite his reservations about the menu, Jackson was pleased with the evening because Dukakis had asked him if he wanted to be vice president, which Jackson took as a sign he was being given serious consideration by the candidate. It wasn't true, of course, but the civil rights leader's managers reported he was delighted.

All of this set the stage for more discord when, a few days before the convention at Atlanta, Dukakis decided on Senator Lloyd Bentsen of Texas to be the vice presidential nominee. Because of a staff mistake that resulted in a missed telephone call, Jackson learned about the decision not from Dukakis but from reporters who greeted him when he arrived at Washington National Airport on a flight from Cincinnati.

The hypersensitive Jackson wasn't willing to let the mistake pass as the kind of thing that could happen in any campaign. Instead, he chose to infer that it was a racial comment, as did some of his most prominent supporters. The story of the "slight" was given widespread attention, and Jackson kept it alive. Speaking to the National Association for the Advancement of Colored People, he said, "I may not be on the ticket, but I'm qualified. . . . I am expected to register, motivate, and deliver more votes than any congressman alive, and for that work, there must be partnership, equity, and shared responsibility." When Dukakis addressed the same NAACP meeting the next day, delegates greeted him with signs and shouts of "Why not Jesse?"

Jackson continued to pick at the sore points in the relationship with Dukakis and the party. He complained loudly and repeatedly about language in the platform and the makeup of the Democratic National Committee, issues of no conceivable interest to most voters or even most political junkies. In Atlanta he eventually forced a "summit" with the candidate that reinforced the perception that Dukakis was giving him special treatment. In fact, Jackson came away having won no important concessions, but it didn't look that way on the television screens Americans were watching.

Clinton, who apparently had been running for president while still eating strained peas and carrots, had followed the two campaigns closely. He knew that, if he could not be on the ticket, Jackson wanted at least to be "in the room" when campaign decisions were made. But the Arkansas governor also knew he couldn't win without those Reagan Democrats whose attitudes on race might have left something to be desired.

His campaign played the race card as subtly as possible in ways that attracted less attention from the press than they deserved. For example, the Clinton television commercials stressing an end to "welfare as we know it" were broadcast most intensively in the South where the code would be immediately understood. And when the campaign scheduled a meeting at a black event, it usually chose a time too late in the day for the television networks to broadcast it on the evening news programs. Or the candidate would appear at a black college early in the day, then follow quickly with some highly photogenic event that the networks could not resist using in those all-important network-news programs.

The black leaders supporting Clinton, as pragmatic as their white counterparts, were not offended. All that mattered in their view was getting George Bush out of the White House. Twelve years of Republicans had been hard to abide.

So when Jackson came to a meeting of the U.S. Conference of Mayors in Houston still steaming about Clinton's lack of respect at the Rainbow Coalition meeting, his old friend and 1984 campaign chairman, Maynard Jackson of Atlanta, told him to quit whining about Clinton. As he noted, none of the other black mayors had joined in the complaint. It was time to move on. Happily for Clinton, Jesse Jackson refused to do so, thus keeping the story alive into the fall campaign. Again, however, the true story didn't receive the attention it deserved except in a few of the best newspapers.

The lack of honesty and candor on race and politics was even more evident twelve years later when the Reverend Al Sharpton put himself into the equation. Lacking any credentials except a smart mouth, he ran for the Democratic presidential nomination almost solely on the strength of his celebrity and despite a personal history that would have disqualified any other candidate.

Sharpton first appeared on the national stage in New York in 1987 when he took up the cause of a black teenager, Tawana Brawley, who claimed she had been raped by a pack of six white policemen, smeared with dog feces, and stuffed into a trash bag. Local television and the tabloids loved the story, and there was this smooth-talking black guy on the home screens every night spouting inflammatory rhetoric as the controversy boiled on. Indeed, it is probably fair to say Sharpton was a creation of local television and a prime example of its tremendous influence. Once he became the established champion of Tawana Brawley, demanding investigations and blaming racism, even the so-called "mainstream" newspapers were obliged to pay attention to him. Even the good, gray *New York Times.*

In the end, a grand jury found that the whole thing was a hoax, a total fabrication. The teenager had invented the story apparently because she feared her parents' anger after she stayed away from home for several days. Sharpton, however, never quite brought himself to admit he had been taken over the jumps. Nor did he apologize to those he had been damning on local television for weeks. At one point he was convicted by a jury of defaming an assistant district attorney by naming him as one of those who had abused Tawana. The young prosecutor won a financial judgment, but there never was any admission of guilt from Sharpton.

But Sharpton had established himself as a celebrity. And for the New York media, that stature, in turn, meant television and newspaper coverage as he showed up in one "situation" after another, replicating at the local level what Jesse Jackson had done nationally by positioning himself before the cameras on every possible newsworthy occasion. If there was a riot in Crown Heights, the one "leader" sure to be quoted was Al Sharpton. If there was a brawl ending a march in Bensonhurst, guess who was leading the way? If there was a funeral for a black riot victim, who was there to comfort the family and say a few words?

Sharpton clearly enjoyed the attention he could command. When a reporter for *The Washington Post* suggested he was running for president to attract attention to himself, he replied: "There's never been a news cycle that I wasn't in. I don't need to run to be in this news cycle."

And he equally relished the political clout he enjoyed thanks to the news media making him so influential. He boasted that Colin Powell returned his telephone calls, and in 2000 both Al Gore, running for president, and Hillary Rodham Clinton, running for the Senate, felt obliged to call on him in person. The fact that he had been defeated by wide margins in campaigns for both the Senate and mayor of New York apparently did not lessen his ability to be a player in major campaigns.

The lesson in all this is, of course, that simply appearing on television often enough can make anyone who commands attention a celebrity, even someone who, according to former Mayor Ed Koch, should be called Al Charlatan. And that stature, in itself, can lead someone to run for president and can force his party leaders to treat him as a serious candidate when privately they are appalled at the prospect of his candidacy and what it says about the Democratic Party.

Sharpton finally was put in his place by African-American voters who demonstrated in the South Carolina primary in February 2004 that they were serious enough about using their ballots not to waste them on a standup comedian. His below 10 percent finish in a primary in which he campaigned intensely was a humiliating rejection, although Sharpton kept insisting his candidacy had to be kept alive because of the "message" he brought to the Democratic debate. It was the kind of racist rationale that would have brought the house down on any white Democratic candidate.

Few politicians are willing to talk about race with the bluntness that is required to face up to racism. On the whole they are less committed to ending racism than to learning to duck around it or to exploit it. That is why it was noteworthy when former Senator Bill Bradley, seeking the Democratic nomination in 2000, listed race relations among the four or five prime concerns of his candidacy when other party leaders were silent on the subject.

Asked if this was not a counterintuitive gesture, Bradley replied, "I can't believe most Democrats won't agree with this." Then he shrugged and added: "Or that's what I think, anyway." But it has never been a case of agreeing on the evils of racism; instead it is one of being willing to confront the issue directly and become identified with that position.

For Bradley and other politicians who have had a career in professional sports—Republican Jack Kemp is another example—talking about race in a positive way seems to come easy. Perhaps it is their experience of relying on black teammates long before they ran for office. Quarterback Kemp depended on black linemen to block for him, and "Dollar Bill" Bradley played on that great Knicks team with Willis Reed and Walt Frazier. It is no wonder former athletes are not easily intimidated by black politicians.

As it turned out, we would never learn if Bradley's faith was justified. He lost the nomination to Al Gore for other reasons, principally the strategic gaffe of trying to compete in the Iowa caucuses.

Just how many votes are cast in American elections on the basis of racism is impossible to nail down, although pollsters universally agree there is a small but measurable and possibly pivotal group.

A 1989 gubernatorial election in Virginia is often cited as one indicator. Democrat L. Douglas Wilder, a black politician of long experience in the state, defeated a Republican opponent, J. Marshall Coleman, by a single percentage point after the final round of opinion polls showed Wilder leading by at least 10 percent. Indeed, by most professional reckonings Coleman was such a hapless candidate that Wilder probably should have been expected to win by twenty points.

The theory, an article of faith in political lore, is that Wilder's margin fell so far short of the survey figures because so many respondents lied to the poll takers. They were unwilling to vote for a black candidate but equally unwilling to admit it to anyone else. One analysis suggested it might be as many as 8 or 9 percent of Democrats, judging by the Coleman voters who disagreed with the Republican on all the divisive issues in the campaign and might have been expected to vote for Wilder.

Whatever the figure, pollsters agree on the difficulty involved in polling when a black candidate is involved. Among other things, this phenomenon can mislead black politicians who believe on the basis of polls that they can win a statewide election in a state like Georgia or Missouri, only to discover that they have been led astray.

There is other evidence of a racial element in voting patterns in the states, usually but not always in the South. There is a tipping point at which the share of a state's electorate made up of black voters affects the share of the white electorate that a liberal Democrat, black or white, can expect to win in the election. The result is that what looks easy is quite the opposite.

In a state like South Carolina, for example, blacks may make up about 25 percent of the vote, almost all for the Democrat, who as a result needs only one third of the white vote to have a majority. But the experience in presidential elections over the last two generations has been that with states in which white candidates need only 30 to 35 percent of the white vote, they almost always fall short. By contrast, in states where the black share of the electorate is smaller—let's say 12 or 15 percent—the same candidate can find it easier to draw the 38 or 40 percent of whites needed to win.

This is a pattern that can be overcome when one group or the other seems to have a compelling stake in the election and turns out accordingly. The 1997 gubernatorial election in Louisiana was a case in point, pitting the legendary Democratic rogue Edwin Edwards against professed racist and Nazi sympathizer David Duke, running as a Republican to the great chagrin of the national party.

Seldom has an election caused as much panic in the streets. Virtually every public or private entity imaginable—churches, civic organizations, service clubs, real estate developers, business groups, local government officials, labor unions, chambers of commerce—declared their opposition to Duke. Even sportswriters joined in, writing columns about how the Super Bowl would never come to the Superdome in New Orleans if David Duke were governor. Bumper stickers read: VOTE FOR THE CROOK. If you followed the final week of that campaign, you would agree the sky was falling.

The most fearful group of voters were, unsurprisingly, the black citizens of Louisiana faced with the possibility of a former Ku Klux Klan grand wizard as governor. So they voted in huge numbers. Shortly before noon of Election Day, I drove through several black precincts in New Orleans and found the turnout in those neighborhoods already over 90 percent. The streets were lined with young mothers pushing their children's strollers toward the voting booths. No one was going to miss this one.

The result was that Edwin Edwards, rogue or not, won with 61 percent to 39 for Duke.

But before the liberals could congratulate themselves about what a great country this is, analyses of the results showed that 56 percent of whites and 60 percent of non-Catholic whites voted for Duke. And surely no one could claim they didn't know for whom—and for what—they were voting.

Edwards eventually encountered a jury he could not charm and was convicted of a crime. But people still go to New Orleans and the Saints still play in the Superdome.

The problem of dealing with race in politics is centered almost entirely among the Democrats. They are the ones who need to rely on the black turnout and the 85 to 90 percent solidity of the black vote. When turnout is down, the Republicans prosper as they did in 1994 in capturing both houses of Congress. The Democrats know that neither Carter nor Clinton would have been elected without the margin black voters provided in southern states and several major industrial-belt states.

Some Democrats argue privately that the party would be better in the long run if it was less wedded to its African-American supporters—and perceived as such by a wider cross section of the white electorate. But even if such a transformation were a good idea, which it isn't, it would require several elections, when for all politicians it is the next one that counts.

And the fact is that within the Democratic Party African-American political operatives are gaining influence that goes far beyond gestures or tokenism. After the Dukakis defeat in 1988, the late Ronald H. Brown became the first black chairman of the Democratic National Committee and laid the foundation for the party's comeback in 1992. He overcame some stiff resistance to win the chairmanship, but after watching his performance in the job, those who had resisted him became enthusiastic admirers.

Several black women rose to powerful positions during the Clinton years. Alexis Herman served on the White House staff and then in the cabinet. Minyon Moore became the chief political adviser in the White House. And Donna Brazile served as manager of Al Gore's 2000 presidential campaign without being to blame for the outcome.

The Republicans give lip service to their intention to broaden their party and bring in more blacks, and some of them are serious enough about it that it costs them the support of the most conservative whites. Kemp, to cite the most obvious case, was viewed with some suspicion by many fellow Republicans who agreed with his conservative positions on issues but were put off by his aggressive attempts to broaden the party. The days of the progressive eastern liberal establishment, or "Rockefeller wing," have long since passed.

Instead, it is Republicans who are playing on racial resentments in the rawest and most divisive way. It was a Republican senator, Jesse Helms, who ran a racist television commercial attacking affirmative action when his reelection seemed threatened by a black Democrat, Harvey Gantt, the former mayor of Charlotte. It showed the white hands of a worker crumbling a piece of paper, putatively a notice that he had lost a job to a black because of affirmative action. It was a Republican presidential candidate, George H. W. Bush, whose campaign ran the infamous Willie Horton commercial against Michael S. Dukakis in 1988. It showed a black murderer who had committed a violent crime on a weekend furlough from a Massachusetts prison.

The Republicans also seem to have a genius for alienating black voters with their legislative proposals and, surprisingly often, with campaign ploys that fool no one and frequently evoke a backlash. Over the last thirty years, in states as diverse as Arizona, New Jersey, Louisiana, and Virginia, they have tried to discourage black turnout by, for example, sending certified letters to all voters in black precincts warning them that they will have to meet some rigid criteria if they want to cast their ballots.

When supporters of Republican W. Henson Moore tried that old chestnut against Democratic Senator John Breaux in Shreveport, Louisiana, local Republicans with impeccable conservative credentials complained loudly to the press. The time has passed when the respectable burghers of even a bastion of conservative thought such as North Louisiana are all comfortable with such tactics.

The Republican complaint, obviously valid, is that the Democrats pander to African-American voters, who in turn expect special treatment. It is impossible to argue with either of those propositions. It is equally valid, however, to say that it is the Republicans who exploit and encourage racism among white voters. This is not true of all Republicans, by any means, and perhaps not of a majority of Republicans. But the ones stirring up bad feeling among white voters are usually Republican.

And when it comes to pandering to the black community, the all-time champion was a Republican, the patrician George Herbert Walker Bush. He chose Clarence Thomas for the Supreme Court. That one retired the cup.

9

SOUND AND FURY, SIGNIFYING A GOTCHA!

*I*n early April 1976 Jimmy Carter, well ahead of the pack in his quest for the Democratic presidential nomination, was asked by Sam Roberts of the New York *Daily News* what he thought about building public housing on scattered sites in the suburbs, an issue then being debated by those who imagined public housing could have some social utility beyond putting a roof over the heads of the poor.

Carter replied that he would favor a plan "oriented primarily where the housing is needed most—downtown areas of deteriorating cities. There's a need to protect the family entity, the neighborhood. I don't think I would do anything to cause deterioration of neighborhoods."

"Well," Roberts went on, "can a black central city survive surrounded by all-white neighborhoods?"

"Yes," said Carter. "My next-door neighbor is black. It hasn't hurt us—provided you give people the freedom to decide for themselves where to live. But to artificially inject another racial group in a community? I see nothing wrong with ethnic purity being maintained. I would not force a racial integration of a neighborhood by government action. But I would not permit discrimination moving into the neighborhood."

Neither Roberts nor the editors of his newspaper saw anything striking about this. The candidate's comments seemed well within the bounds of normal political discourse and, perhaps more important, seemed totally consistent with the prevailing dogma in the Democratic Party. So it would seem appropriate that Carter's remarks appeared in the sixteenth paragraph of a nineteen-paragraph story that ran way back with the truss ads in the Sunday edition of the *News.* It was no big deal.

But a CBS News editor, obviously hypersensitive to violations of political correctness even before the term was invented, spotted what he decided was an offending phrase, "ethnic purity." He alerted a CBS reporter, who quickly questioned Carter about it at a press conference the following day, a public enough occasion to put the "issue" into the public domain and the pack of reporters on the case.

Explaining his choice of words, Carter even repeated the putatively offensive phrase. He said: "I have nothing against a community that's made up of people who are Polish, Czechoslovakians, French Canadians, or blacks who are trying to maintain the ethnic purity of their neighborhood. This is a natural inclination on the part of people." He added, however, the critical caveat: "I would never, though, condone any sort of discrimination against, say, a black family or another family from moving into that neighborhood."

Some of the liberals who had always distrusted Carter because he was a southerner now began crowing that they finally had the evidence to justify their doubts. For all the talk about his special rapport with black Americans, he was talking about "ethnic purity." Maybe he was just another racist cracker after all.

The whole thing was nonsense, of course. Carter had a closer relationship with blacks than either of his prime rivals for the nomination at that point in the campaign, Representative Morris Udall of Arizona and Senator Henry Jackson of Washington. Neither was a racist either, but neither had many blacks among his constituents. The demographics were all wrong. And Udall, because he was brought up a Mormon, in a church in which blacks were not welcomed, had an added burden in building trust with many African Americans.

Nonsense or not, such instant controversies seem to have a life of their own. Those who wanted to deny Carter the presidential nomination before he nailed it down were quick to exploit what they saw as an opening. And reporters were in full cry, trying to "advance the story" by coming up with some "new angle" the competition could not match. The press was quick to remind the voters that Carter had not always been an outspoken champion of racial integration as a Georgia politician. That was one of the "new angles," of course.

The operative question, the one that mattered politically, was whether the phrase was so offensive to black Americans that their leaders would now turn away from Carter and perhaps even cost him the nomination. Most of those from Georgia, prominently including Andrew Young, had endorsed Carter, the one notable exception being Julian Bond. The supportive views of those closest to the candidate were not enough, however, to measure the effect of his advocacy of "ethnic purity." It sounded like something a Nazi might say, for heaven's sake, and those delicate liberal ears were burning.

I was covering the campaign for the *Washington Star* when the story burst onto the national scene. I can recall that, perhaps being short on sensitivity, I was puzzled about how to assess the political damage, if any, Carter had suffered. Facing an afternoon newspaper deadline only an hour away, I called city hall in Detroit and asked Mayor Coleman Young's press secretary if I could get the black mayor, a notoriously outspoken free spirit, on the telephone to enlist his views on "ethnic purity." A few minutes later the mayor returned my call and cleared up the whole question in a single sentence.

"Ethnic purity," he said, "is as American as Mom's apple pie."

The message to me was that Carter probably could ride out the instant brouhaha without suffering any lasting political wounds. If a hard case like Coleman Young was staying with him, he had little to fear from potential defectors of far less political weight.

But Carter still was obliged by the rules of politics and journalism to put the question to rest so the press and his rivals would stop harp-

ing on it. That effort took several days in which Carter grew increasingly testy as reporters kept asking the same questions in different ways.
He was doing what most politicians under pressure seem to do: blame
the messengers in the press. Reporters who have been around the track
a few times expect and accept such responses without getting all bent
out of shape. But more often complaints from the victim of a Gotcha!
only stir up the animals with their little notebooks and make them
even more aggressive in seeking out new angles.

Carter finally conceded in a notably and understandably grudging
apology that his "unfortunate use of the term 'ethnic purity' " had
been a mistake. He had been "careless" and guilty of "an improper
choice of words," he said. That was about as far as Jimmy Carter would
grovel, but in the end it was far enough. The campaign arranged a
noontime rally in downtown Atlanta where the Reverend Martin
Luther King, Sr., father of the fallen civil rights leader, delivered his
blessing in unrestrained language. Describing Carter as "a man I have
loved and believed in," the elder King praised the candidate for his
apologies and told a cheering, largely black crowd, "So, Governor, I'm
with you all the way." The television cameras were there in force, so
for the Carter campaign it was time to relax. The crisis, if that is what
it was, had passed.

Although the term had not come into the political lexicon by this
time, the "ethnic purity" story was the quintessential example of the
Gotcha!—the news story raising questions about a politician's personal
history or views on sensitive issues or, worse yet, the dreaded "flip-
flop." Politicians, unlike the rest of us, are not permitted to change
their minds on any question that might be considered politically sensitive by, in the case of Democrats, some querulous picky-picky liberal
on the West Side or, in the case of Republicans, some Bible-thumping
fundamentalist in Oklahoma. Forget about Emerson's "foolish consis-
tency."

The Gotcha! usually centers on issues or events that the press and
political community think are important even if the voters may be
scratching their heads and wondering why. These are the questions
that, though often inconsequential, set off what has become known as

a "firestorm" or a "feeding frenzy" in the press. Sharks in the water smelling blood and all that stuff, the whole compendium of clichés for use on such occasions.

The basic ingredients are almost always the same. The cause of the Gotcha! is usually something that can be captured by the press in a single word or phrase, such as "ethnic purity." Most often the story centers on something that seems to reveal an already suspected chink in the candidate's armor. The original story is followed by much hand wringing and viewing with faux alarm by the candidate's rivals. The candidate is at first baffled by the whole furor and resists offering the apology or explanation recommended by his advisers, who are in a panic because their tiger has put his foot in his mouth but nobody wants to tell him. The candidate finally decides to square the whole thing but only after growing angry with the press for fomenting the damned crisis. On the op-ed page, some political scientist explains the deeper meaning of the controversy—perhaps, as George Corley Wallace used to say, the trauma resulted "because his daddy never carried him to a Pittsburgh Steelers game."

Meanwhile, the voters, at least most of them, are puzzled about the episode, although they suspect it does not reflect well on the candidate. The voters also seem to know that most of these alarums and excursions by the press and politicians have little relevance to their lives. They rarely have anything to do with creating more decent jobs, educating children, treating the old and poor with some respect, or protecting the environment.

In short, the distinguishing characteristic of the Gotcha! is that the issue it raises is usually trivial except in the eyes of a few people in politics and the press.

There are, of course, some occasions when one of these brief but intense controversies tells all of us—meaning press and voters—something we should know about the candidate. The lessons can even be positive. In the case of Carter and "ethnic purity," we learned that he was determined enough to win that he was willing to put aside his not inconsiderable pride and explain himself. And we learned that his rapport with black leaders and black Americans in general was as strong as his supporters had claimed all along. It was an advantage his rivals for the Democratic nomination, even including Udall with his spotless liberal voting record in Congress, could not match.

More often, however, the results of these excursions into rhetorical extravagance and factual exaggeration by the press and politicians are not positive, even if the damage is limited.

Howard Dean, for example, was nailed in a Gotcha! when, as the putative hot property among Democratic presidential aspirants in late 2003, he said out loud that he wanted to appeal to whites in the South who have Confederate flags in their pickup trucks. What he meant is that he wanted to reach those socially conservative Democrats who had left the party for Republicans—Ronald Reagan twice and George H. W. Bush once in the 1980s. These were the same Democrats Bill Clinton wooed with great success in winning the White House in 1992.

No one who knew anything about either Dean or the Democratic contest had any reason to believe the former governor of Vermont was a racist. All the evidence had been to the contrary. But most of his competitors, all trailing far behind him in the contest for the nomination at the time, went into a breast-beating frenzy of recrimination about how morally indefensible his position had become until he finally backed off and apologized for his use of the language if not for his political intent.

He made his apologies in a peevish way, however. And his explanation of his intentions sounded as if he was talking down to these white southerners. He sounded like just another elitist liberal prescribing the best medicine for everyone else.

Thus, although the flap was unfair to Dean to the extent that it raised any question about his racial attitudes, it was nonetheless revealing of an extraordinary self-assurance that could easily be mistaken for arrogance.

There was no similar benefit of the doubt granted Senator Trent Lott of Mississippi, then the majority leader, when he blundered into the thicket of race in 2002. At a birthday party for Senator Strom Thurmond of South Carolina, Lott recalled Thurmond's campaign for president in 1948 as the candidate of the segregationist Dixiecrats. If Thurmond had won that election, Lott rambled on, "we wouldn't have had all these problems over the years."

There was little reason to wonder what "all these problems" might have been, despite Lott's fervent denial of any racist intent. Indeed, the Gotcha! set off such a wild season of what now passes for political debate that he was forced to step down as majority leader. The suspicion among his critics was that this was one of those slips of the tongue that reveal the common conversation in the locker room—such as when House Majority Leader Richard Armey of Texas referred to Representative Barney Frank of Massachusetts, who is openly homosexual, as "Barney Fag." Nobody believed Armey had misspoken.

Frequently a Gotcha! dies a quick and natural death for lack of sustenance from the press or politician's rivals. In 1968, for example, the Republican candidate for vice president, Spiro T. Agnew, was cited for referring to a Japanese-American reporter for the Baltimore *Sun,* Gene Oishi, as "the fat Jap." But Agnew knew Oishi as a reporter who covered his state administration in Annapolis, and he used the phrase, uttered in private and in passing, in a good-humored way that fit the tough kidding that was common on campaign planes in those days. And besides, Agnew already had built a reputation as a politically clumsy clod likely to put his foot in his mouth, as he did by calling a Pole a "Polack." So harping on this one gaffe was gilding the lily. As it turned out, once he took office his lack of sensitivity reached a level that allowed him to accept one-hundred-dollar bills in a plain brown envelope in the vice president's office. What a guy.

Similarly, President George H. W. Bush escaped any serious harm when intrepid reporters seized on his reference to his grandchildren as "the little brown ones." The "story" apparently was that Bush was revealing some ethnic or racial attitude, but it was too preposterous to last more than a couple of news cycles. The grandchildren's mother, Columba Bush, wife of Governor Jeb Bush of Florida, was a Latin American, so their complexion was hardly surprising. And in any case, whatever else was wrong with George Bush (plenty in my view), he was not a racist.

Tom Foley, a respected congressman from Washington and the Democratic majority leader in 1989, was the favored candidate to replace Speaker Jim Wright of Texas, who was being forced out of Congress on a conflict-of-interest charge. But some Democratic critics and some Republicans had been circulating rumors that Foley was a homosexual—rumors without any foundation—and thus too much of a risk to be Speaker. The story finally exploded when a Republican National Committee publication compared Foley's voting record with that of the openly gay Representative Barney Frank under the headline OUT OF THE LIBERAL CLOSET.

That tore it, and the Republicans were forced to fire the RNC staff member responsible. But the political noise was so loud for a few days that Foley was obliged to appear on television and affirm his heterosexuality.

There are times when the hypocrisy involved in a Gotcha! goes far beyond even the usual tolerant standards of politics. That was the case when it was revealed that Douglas Ginsburg, a Harvard professor nominated for the Supreme Court, was known to his students and colleagues as an enthusiastic marijuana user. The furor had some justification, of course. It is hard to make a case for someone who breaks the law being chosen for the highest court in the land. And Ginsburg not only smoked pot but did so with students. But his critics clearly included a great many politicians of the same generation who also had used the weed.

Indeed, after his nomination was scuttled, there was a rush of candidates for the Democratic nomination in 1988, including Al Gore and Bruce Babbitt, who confessed to indulging in marijuana, although insisting it was youthful experimentation. And they had enough sense not to claim that they never inhaled.

The cup for hypocrisy might have been retired, however, in a Gotcha! involving Senator John Kerry of Massachusetts when he was running what was then an uphill campaign for the Democratic presidential nomination in 2003. His crime was using a naughty word. Discussing President Bush's policy on Iraq in an interview with *Rolling Stone,* Kerry asked rhetorically, "Did I expect George Bush to fuck it up as badly as he did?"

The morals police were on that one instantly, and the leader of the forces of hypocrisy was Andrew Card, the White House chief of staff, who went on a Sunday-morning television interview show and said with a straight face that he was "very disappointed that he would use that kind of language." It made you wonder how disappointed he was when his own president used the same kind of language from time to time. But the hypocrisy also extended to the press. Why was it news when a politician used the phrase "fuck it up"? Does anyone believe they never talk that way? Does anyone, except perhaps some crackpot preacher, imagine this is a telling indicator of their morality?

There is clearly no requirement that one of these "issues" be either substantial or logical. Seeking the Democratic nomination in 2004, General Wesley Clark found himself standing on a stage when a supporter, film director Michael Moore, described President George W. Bush as a "deserter" from his service in the National Guard during the war in Vietnam. If Clark had been more ring-wise politically, he would have immediately repudiated, or at least distanced himself from, Moore's use of the term, but instead he simply let it pass.

This set off the bloodhounds of the press, who pursued him on the question with vigor both off-camera and, more to the point, during a nationally televised debate leading up to the South Carolina primary. Clark tried to point out that he had not used the term himself and, in fact, didn't agree with it. But still the questions came about why he hadn't disavowed—or perhaps disemboweled—Michael Moore on the spot. The whole thing was, of course, preposterous. Clark had erred politically by not recognizing the pothole, but there was no reason to blame him for Moore's penchant for extravagant rhetoric. After all, another of Clark's Hollywood supporters was Madonna. So, if you follow this logic to its ultimate end, the candidate should have been questioned closely on what he thought about that famous kiss Madonna laid on Britney Spears.

Sometimes the excesses of the press in one of these situations can have a marked impact on the shape of a campaign. In 1972 George McGovern, the Democratic nominee for president, became the victim of a classic Gotcha! He dropped Senator Thomas Eagleton of Missouri as his running mate after saying he was "one thousand percent behind him" despite the disclosure that Eagleton had been treated for emotional problems with electric-shock therapy. The wise guys on television and in the press had a field day with that one, speculating for several days about the proper definition of 1,000 percent and braying about how McGovern had been forced to "flip-flop" on Eagleton.

What was largely missing from the press coverage was any understanding of the wrenching dilemma McGovern faced in weighing political practicality—his chance for the White House—against what many fellow liberals considered an unenlightened view of emotional illness.

In this case the Gotcha! was far less important than the facts of the case. Once McGovern was forced to replace Eagleton, any chance he might have enjoyed of defeating President Richard M. Nixon went up in smoke when the Democratic nominee had to cast around desperately for a replacement before Sargent Shriver, a charming Kennedy in-law who had run the Peace Corps, agreed to join the ticket. The "one thousand percent" remark became a footnote, although one that reflected negatively on McGovern.

For McGovern the most galling thing was that while the Eagleton problem was compromising his campaign beyond repair, neither the electorate nor the press was paying much attention to the unfolding Watergate story.

McGovern was not the first presidential candidate victimized by a Gotcha!

One of the classic cases old—make that very old—reporters still talk about was the fall of Governor George Romney of Michigan when he ran for the Republican presidential nomination in 1968. Romney was a forceful man who had earned a reputation as an industrialist by making a success of American Motors and the Rambler before he entered politics. As a governor he was progressive and effective enough, as well as personally attractive enough, to be a realistic presidential candidate. So early in 1967 he began testing the waters and earning a clearly positive response from potential voters and the press.

But Romney had not grown up in politics and didn't understand fully all the "rules" by which the game is played. Thus, he wandered into trouble when he began criticizing the policies of President Lyndon B. Johnson in promulgating the war in Vietnam without offering his own prescriptions for a new policy. For several months those of us covering him regularly—and acting as the self-appointed champions of fairness—picked at him, demanding his plan for the war as a necessary prerequisite for someone who wanted to criticize Johnson. But Romney resisted, protesting that his policies would be unveiled at the proper time.

This tug-of-war continued for months without any indication that most Americans were paying much attention. They may have had a vague notion that George Romney's position on Vietnam was "controversial"—a word that means whatever you want it to mean in politics—but that was about all they knew. Romney's critics, mostly conservative Republicans who saw him as a watered-down Nelson Rockefeller progressive, were questioning whether he was capable of producing a plan. After all, he was an automobile manufacturer and a state official. What the hell did he know about national security?

In late summer, however, Romney fell victim to a destructive Gotcha! that crystallized the doubts. In an interview about the war on a Detroit radio station, he complained that when he visited Vietnam to see for himself, he had been "brainwashed." That tore it. This was the evidence the press and political community needed to prove George Romney was out of his depth. He was even admitting he had been conned. How can you elect someone that gullible to the White House? How can you have a president who's been brainwashed? Negative judgments on the hapless Romney were handed down right and left.

However, no one with any weight in the news media—not newspapers and certainly not television—bothered to examine what Romney was saying. He was not conceding that he had been persuaded to accept a false view of what was happening in Vietnam. That is what everyone inferred from the usual meaning of the term *brainwashed*—a change of mind or an acceptance of ideas heretofore unacceptable. Instead, Romney was saying that the military leaders and diplomats he encountered in Vietnam tried to sell him a bill of goods that he knew to be false.

The distinction was one that could not be made in the crude rhetoric of a political debate. He had been brainwashed, he was out of his depth, end of story. By the time he came forward with a detailed plan for "de-Americanizing" the war, a plan remarkably similar to the one President Richard M. Nixon later followed, his political stock had gone through the floor. His views on the pressing and complex problems of the cities, the economy, race—all were essentially ignored. Whatever Romney did was seen through the prism of Vietnam. It wasn't fair; he was better than that.

But politics often isn't fair. Romney's position was so thoroughly compromised that his campaign imploded. He fell so far behind in the New Hampshire primary contest with the "new" Nixon that he decided to abandon his campaign entirely and go home to Lansing before the first ballots were cast. The only obstacles on Nixon's path to the nomination were last-gasp and ineffectual challenges from two Republican progressives, Governors William Scranton of Pennsylvania and Nelson A. Rockefeller of New York.

The ramifications of a Gotcha! are sometimes unpredictable and unintended. A case in point was a celebrated "attack video" controversy that compromised any chance Senator Joe Biden of Delaware might have had for the Democratic nomination in 1988—and, quite incidentally, crippled the campaign of the eventual winner of the nomination, Governor Michael S. Dukakis of Massachusetts.

This one grew out of a television commercial that Neil Kinnock, leader of the Labour Party in Great Britain, was using to great applause in his campaign against Prime Minister Margaret Thatcher. In the spot, Kinnock is shown giving a speech in which he asks: "Why am I the first Kinnock in a thousand generations to be able to get to university? Why is Glenys [his wife, seated in the audience] the first woman in her family in a thousand generations to get to university? Was it because all our predecessors were thick?"

Then he asks why his forebears who were Welsh coal miners hadn't succeeded as he had. "Did they lack talent? Those people who could sing and play and recite and write poetry. Those people who could make wonderful, beautiful things with their hands. Those people who could dream dreams, see visions. Why didn't they get it? Was it because they were weak? Those people who could work eight hours underground and then come up to play football? Weak? Does anybody really think that they didn't get what we had because they didn't have the talent or the strength or the endurance or the commitment? Of course not. It was because there was no platform on which they could stand."

Biden had been given a tape of the Kinnock commercial and was so impressed that he began to use his own version of the speech, usually but not always attributing it to the British politician. Several reporters had heard him do so and even mentioned Kinnock in their stories. But when Biden used it in August at the Iowa State Fair, he failed to mention Kinnock and his language suggested it was his own.

He put it this way: "I started thinking as I was coming over here, why is it that Joe Biden is the first in his family ever to go to a university? Why is it that my wife, who is sitting out there in the audience, is the first in her family ever to go to college? Is it because our fathers and mothers were not bright? Is it because I'm the first Biden in a thousand generations to get a college and a graduate degree that I was smarter than the rest? Those same people who read poetry and wrote poetry and taught me how to sing verse? Is it because they didn't work hard? My ancestors who worked in the coal mines of northeastern Pennsylvania and would come up after twelve hours and play football for four hours? No, it's not because they weren't as smart. It's not because they didn't work as hard. It's because they didn't have a platform on which to stand."

The appropriation of Kinnock's rhetoric was obvious. But on those earlier occasions and some subsequent ones, Biden had given Kinnock some credit for the speech without being too careful about the authenticity of the autobiographical comparison he implied. Biden did not come from a long line of coal miners—his father was an automobile dealer in Wilmington—although his staff tried to insist he could at least claim the family came from Scranton, capital of anthracite mining. So the fact was that Biden was adopting not only Kinnock's rhetoric but his persona.

On the face of it, Biden's transgression didn't seem to be a political felony, only another example of a politician living off the land, exploiting every opportunity and stretching the truth. But the context made it far more damaging than it might otherwise have been.

Most important, perhaps, was the timing. This came up only a few months after the flaming controversy over Gary Hart and Donna Rice that had forced the front-runner for the 1988 nomination to the sidelines. So the "character issue," as it was called, now was a preoccupation for reporters covering the early stages of the campaign. No one wanted to be the last on the beat to find the really juicy stuff that might disqualify a candidate.

The second critical element in the context was the fact that most of the reporters covering the campaign didn't know Biden very well. As he pointed out after the fact, he had spent much of his time in the Senate commuting daily to Wilmington, only ninety minutes away, to be with his family, so he had no history of frequent schmoozing with reporters or other politicians. The one thing we knew about Joe Biden as a potential presidential nominee was that he could deliver a crowd-pleasing red-faced speech to a Democratic Party rally. Now there were questions about the authenticity of that rhetoric as a political asset.

Inevitably, reporters were soon tipped to other episodes in Biden's career that suggested he was inclined to exaggeration and plagiarism long before the Neil Kinnock speech caught his fancy. Some of these might have been written off as the mistakes of youth. But there were enough examples that they were seen in the political community as a pattern of dishonesty, and the consensus was broad enough that Biden folded his campaign.

(As it turned out, the episode may have saved Biden's life. Running for the nomination, he had been suffering headaches—unusual for him—that were severe enough that at one point he was forced to interrupt a speech to a Rotary Club in Nashua for fifteen minutes. At first Biden chalked up his problems to the tensions of the campaign.

But a few months after his withdrawal he suffered two brain aneurysms that almost killed him, leading to several months in the hospital before he made a recovery that permitted him to return to the Senate. It is reasonable to doubt he would have survived if he had still been an active candidate.)

The end of Biden's candidacy was not the end of the matter, however. This was an episode with unintended consequences that claimed a second victim, Michael Dukakis. And it was here that the press failed to put the incident into its proper context and treat it with some sense of proportion.

The issue now became finding who was responsible for bringing down Joe Biden by distributing the video showing both the original Kinnock and the Biden version.

Unsurprisingly, Biden's unhappy supporters were quick to call the whole thing an example of political "dirty tricks" akin to those used by the infamous CREEP—the Committee to Re-Elect the President—that earned so much attention in Richard Nixon's 1972 campaign. So the hunt was on for the culprits who "leaked" the video to *The New York Times* and *The Des Moines Register,* the two newspapers that broke the story.

In truth, there was nothing wrong with any campaign calling attention to such a clearly questionable action by a rival candidate. At the very same time the George H. W. Bush campaign on the Republican side was shedding crocodile tears about the Democratic dirty tricks, the Bush agents were also telephoning political reporters like me to tell us about something potentially damaging that Bob Dole, Bush's main rival for the nomination, had said in Wisconsin. In case we had missed our copy of the Milwaukee *Sentinel* that morning, ha ha, they were delivering by messenger envelopes of clippings that reflected poorly on Dole. The Dole campaign did the same kind of thing, as did all the Democratic campaigns. It is called "negative research," and there is absolutely nothing unethical or "dirty" about it.

There were, however, special circumstances in this case. In his report on Biden's use of the Kinnock speech, David Yepsen, the *Register*'s all-star political reporter, called it an "attack video" and said it had been given to him by a rival campaign that he did not identify. This bit of colorful prose, as well as responsible reporting on the source, turned the attention of the scandal hunters to the "dirty tricks" issue that was really no issue at all.

The instant conventional wisdom in the press and political community pointed to the campaign of Richard Gephardt, the House Democratic leader from neighboring Missouri who was favored to win the Iowa precinct caucuses that year but perhaps was growing edgy about gains Biden appeared to be making. There were several theories, one being that some consultants to Gephardt were simply trying to get revenge against the mercurial Pat Caddell, the consultant to Biden. There is always a market for arcane conspiracy theories in political campaigns—and many newsrooms—and most of them are unfounded, as was the case here.

When attention turned to Dukakis, the candidate responded with his characteristic certitude. "Anybody who knows me and knows the kind of campaigns I run knows how strongly I feel about negative campaigning," he said. Even after twenty years in politics, the usually perceptive Dukakis didn't recognize the difference between "dirty tricks" and legitimate political actions. He was still nourishing the prissy attitudes he apparently acquired in the genteel politics of afternoon coffees with Brookline liberals.

The problem, of course, was that the "attack video" had been put together by John Sasso, the campaign manager and closest adviser to the Massachusetts governor. And it had been given to the *Times*, the *Register*, and NBC News by Sasso and Paul Tully, the campaign's brilliant political director who had first spotted the effectiveness of Biden's rhetoric at that Iowa appearance without knowing about the Kinnock model.

The fatal flaw in their strategy had been their failure to simply call a press conference and publicly show the videotape, leaving it up to the reporters to draw all the damaging inferences. Or they could have simply owned up to having passed along the video and defended their actions. The issue would have been what was shown on the tape, not who disclosed it. There would have been no comparisons to CREEP and no "attack video" phrase for the television networks to seize as they drummed away at the story in their usual shorthand way. But because they waited to be "exposed," the embarrassed Dukakis decided there was no alternative except to apologize to Biden and fire both Sasso and Tully.

It was an extremely costly decision. Sasso, although brought back to the campaign after the primaries, left a huge gap because of his close personal and special relationship with Dukakis. Tully, who died during the Clinton campaign four years later, was probably the single most perceptive strategist among Democratic professionals of the time. The loss to Dukakis, who tended to blame "hired gun" Tully for the whole fiasco, is impossible to quantify. But Dukakis came close enough in the general election, losing by only four percentage points after a flawed campaign performance on his own part, that it was reasonable to believe he might have won with Sasso and Tully.

But if the Gotcha! on Dukakis was undeserved, it was revealing. He was a candidate so rigid and upright that even those closest to him were afraid to tell him about the way politics can be hardball, even if totally legitimate tactics are used. It makes you wonder how he would have performed in the White House dealing with the snakes in Congress. But then again, after you see how George H. W. Bush performed, the prospect seems less daunting. It's the great thing about this country: The system is strong enough to survive an empty suit for four years.

Another Republican empty suit, Senator Dan Quayle of Indiana, was the victim of the most unrestrained and unfair series of Gotchas! in the 1988 campaign. He was forced to defend himself on essentially inconsequential complaints about his past that he made into issues with his own clumsy use of the language. Again, the context was important.

To begin with, in the days just before the Republican convention opened in New Orleans, both politicians and reporters laughed when they heard Quayle's name was on the list of those Vice President George Bush was considering. He was a senator of no particular distinction and no demonstrable intellectual heft—in New York they would have said, "He's so light he can walk on a charlotte russe"—and he didn't serve any obvious political purpose. If the ticket needed someone from Indiana, which no Republican ticket ever seems to need, why not Senator Richard Lugar, a heavyweight respected throughout the political community?

One puzzled Republican senator not on the Bush list recalled that Quayle had frequently dropped by Bush's office in the Capitol late in the day when the vice president was waiting to see if his vote was needed to break a tie. "He would put his feet up and have a drink with Bush, maybe ask his advice," this senator said. The suggestion, not outlandish to some who knew Bush, was that he might want an acolyte as his running mate, someone who would pose no threat just as he had posed no threat to Ronald Reagan for eight years. Another "lapdog," as that insightful critic of conservative culture, George Will, might have put it.

But Dan Quayle was a candidate with baggage quite beyond light. In 1980 he had been one of several Republican congressmen who shared a vacation house in Florida for a golfing weekend and were joined by Paula Parkinson, a knockout blond lobbyist who had once posed nude for *Playboy* magazine. So far as anyone knew, Quayle was not guilty of any sexual indiscretion. He said he played golf and left the day after Parkinson arrived. And besides, it was no secret that she was the special friend of another House member sharing the weekend who later paid for the relationship by losing his seat in Congress. But the Parkinson-Quayle "story" was going to be fodder for the late-afternoon television scandal shows just coming into their own and for the sensationalist newspapers. In short, considering the national trauma caused by Gary Hart's trip on the *Monkey Business,* that Florida weekend was enough baggage to disqualify many vice presidential possibilities, even if unfairly.

As it turned out, not Dan Quayle. Bush chose him, introduced him to the nation from a riverside wharf in New Orleans, and set off one Gotcha! after another. The newly minted nominee-designate didn't help matters by gamboling around the platform and around Bush like the giddy winner of a washer-dryer in a television game show. The following morning, at a joint press conference with Bush, he showed his handlers and the sharks with the pencils and cameras that there were indeed some rough edges that could cause him trouble.

Asked if it was accurate to say, as his staff had insisted, that he had met Paula Parkinson only once and played golf the rest of the time, a testy Quayle replied, "No"—thus baffling his inquisitors, who asked what, then, was accurate. "That has been covered and there's nothing to it," he shot back. Then there was the question of why, as the Democrats already were asking, "someone who says he's tough on defense" had joined the National Guard in 1969 to avoid going to fight in Vietnam. This one Quayle dismissed as a "cheap shot," but the reporters persisted, of course. There is nothing that inspires the pack quite like blatant hypocrisy. And Quayle the hawk compounded the felony when he reviewed his decision to stay home in the Guard as part of his plan to marry, go to law school, and have a family—and added: "I did not know in 1969 that I would be in this room today." The implication was obvious: If he had known it would help his political career, he would have gone to Vietnam rather than the National Guard. That comment alone was enough to nourish the issue for at least another week or two.

As the Paula Parkinson and Vietnam issues played out, Quayle continued to be the focus of national attention—to the point that the news coverage of the campaign on network television and in major newspapers centered on the Gotchas! for more than two weeks. If Bush or Dukakis had come up with a plan for saving the world, it might well have ended up on page two.

The Guard story was particularly awkward because questions were quickly raised about how he had managed to get a coveted place in the National Guard when so many were trying to hide out there. Quayle came from a wealthy and influential family, owners of the *Indianapolis Star* and *News,* the most powerful newspapers in Indiana, so there was the obvious suspicion that he had had a little help. And the candidate quickly obliged in an interview with Tom Brokaw at the convention hall by suggesting that maybe "phone calls were made" in his behalf.

Then, asked by Dan Rather the same night what his worst fear was, Quayle replied: "Paula Parkinson." It was not the answer most likely to calm the savages or reassure his handlers.

As it turned out, the intrepid reporters learned that in fact "calls were made" by influential people to clear the way into the Guard for the young law student. And Paula Parkinson, in an interview in *Playboy* for which she was paid, filled in some blanks on the Florida weekend by saying that Quayle "flirted" with her, danced "extremely" close—heh, heh, we all know what that means—and "wanted to make love" but was turned down.

In the end it all came to nothing. Although few would admit it, some of the reporters pursuing Quayle were embarrassed to be spending their professional energies on such a third-rate politician. They wanted to show just how callow he was and what a mistake Bush had made in choosing him to be a heartbeat from the presidency. But none of it mattered. Quayle was such a weak candidate that the Bush managers tried to hide him in secondary and tertiary markets on the theory that they were okay in Boise and Terre Haute anyway. And compared with his Democratic opposite number, Lloyd Bentsen, he was a disaster. So what? So nothing. People don't vote for vice president.

There have been Gotcha!s centered on even less consequential matters than whether a vice presidential nominee dodged the draft. Since 1992 that kind of history has become a standard entry in the résumés of our presidents. None, however, was more trivial than the controversy over Jimmy Carter's confession that he harbored lust in his heart from time to time.

The phrase was taken from a series of long interviews conducted in the early summer of 1976 by Robert Scheer, a highly respected writer, as part of several such pieces about presidential candidates that he was doing for *Playboy* magazine. The most politically sensitive questions dealt with how Carter would be affected as president by his strong religious beliefs as a born-again Christian. For example, would his religion's definition of sin influence his selection of judges? In retrospect, it is clear that Carter tried to be forthcoming and discursive in his replies. In a sense, his candor was a compliment to the electorate, suggesting in essence that he wasn't afraid of being judged on what he had to say about his faith and a wide variety of other topics. He gave the kind of replies that only a few politicians today—the kind who don't get nominated—would risk.

The burden of his argument was that the biblical judgment of adultery and homosexuality, among other things, as sins would not control his conduct as a public official. He said, "We don't assume the role of judge and say to another human being, 'You're condemned because you commit sins.' All Christians, all of us, acknowledge that we are sinful and the judgment comes from God, not from another human being.

"As governor of Georgia," he went on, "I tried to shift the emphasis of law enforcement away from victimless crimes. We lessened the penalties on the use of marijuana. We removed alcoholism as a crime and so forth. Victimless crimes, in my opinion, should have a very low priority in terms of enforcing the laws on the books. But as to appointing judges, that would not be the basis on which I'd appoint them. I would choose people who were competent, whose judgment and integrity were sound. I think it would be inappropriate to ask them how they were going to rule on a particular question before I appointed them." It was the kind of reply that might be a useful model for the following generation of fundamentalist Christians who demand litmus tests for judges and their version of morality from everyone else. And it was also the kind of reply that would reassure Jewish voters and liberal Democrats who might be uneasy about having a southern Baptist in the White House. Carter was, after all, a highly skilled politician as well as a Baptist.

However, Scheer and Barry Golson, the *Playboy* editor working with him, wanted to explore other facets of the "religion issue" and asked for one final interview to finish the job. Carter invited them to Plains right after the Democratic convention in July. He described the "autonomy" that was the rule in the Baptist church and his own freedom from religious pressures as a public official. And he summarized his own religiosity in these terms:

"I try not to commit a deliberate sin. I recognize that I'm going to do it anyhow because I am human and I'm tempted. And Christ set some almost impossible standards for us. Christ said, 'I tell you that anyone who looks on a woman with lust has in his heart already committed adultery.' I've looked at a lot of women with lust. I've committed adultery in my heart many times. This is something that God recognizes I will do—and I have done it—and God forgives me for it. But that doesn't mean that I condemn someone who not only looks on a woman with lust but leaves his wife and shacks up with somebody out of wedlock."

The candor of Carter's ruminations was remarkable even for that kinder day when politicians didn't feel they had to weigh every utterance against the chance that they would be misunderstood by the press or translated in the wrong way by political opponents. But *Playboy* knew that a presidential nominee admitting to lust in his heart was newsworthy by the mindless criteria that usually apply. So they offered the story to the *Today* show, and blood was in the water, so the sharks rushed to the scene. In the interview Carter not only had admitted to lusting after women but had actually used the word *screw*—an affront to every decent American, judging by the hysterical reaction of the press. They didn't report that this Baptist had been known to say *fuck,* but rarely, and not in their interview.

The whole episode set some even higher standard for hypocrisy on the part of the press and the politicians who clucked disapprovingly about his terrible language. And of course, there were clutches of ministers willing to be quoted tut-tutting about his language; a few even questioned Carter's credentials as an evangelical Christian.

For ordinary mortals, though, the operative question was: What is this brouhaha all about, anyway? If admitting to lust in your heart is a disqualifier, everyone under ninety is ineligible for the White House. It was precisely the kind of Gotcha! that made politicians increasingly wary and wooden and voters disgusted with the triviality of politics. For reporters covering the whole thing, some of them known to do a little lusting of their own from time to time, it was a bit embarrassing.

Several of us traveling with Carter put the whole thing in a better perspective a little later by, as was our custom in those less militant days, writing a song to the tune of "Heart of My Heart" that went this way:

Lust in my heart, how I love adultery,
Lust in my heart, that's my theology.
When I was young, at the Plains First Baptist Church,
I would preach and sermonize,
But oh, how I would fantasize.
Lust in my heart, who cares if it's a sin,
Leching's a noble art.
It's okay if you shack up,
I won't get my back up,
'Cause I've got mine, I've got lust in my heart.

Lust in my heart, oh, it's bad politically,
Lust in my heart, but it brings publicity.
When I grew up and ran for president,
A bunch of women I did screw—
But in my head so no one knew.
Lust in my heart, I said I'd never lie,
I guess I wasn't smart
But I'm no gay deceiver,
I'm a Christian eager beaver,
As Playboy *said, I've got lust in my heart.*

When we sang the song for Carter at a fifty-second birthday party arranged by his staff in Pittsburgh, both he and Rosalynn laughed hard enough to make us think they enjoyed it. But the whole affair had been anything but a laughing matter for a presidential candidate, as ridiculous as that may be. Imagine that, a real human being, subject sometimes to the baser emotions like all the rest of us, is running for president of the United States! What won't they think of next?

In dwelling on these essentially extraneous subjects, the press has diverted attention and wasted time that might have been better employed to give voters a clearer picture of their candidates' leadership qualities and their agendas for the nation in the next four years. Who knows, the press might even have led a few more people to vote.

10

DEALING WITH SKELETONS

*T*he political press has a hard time dealing with the personal lives of politicians. We don't seem to know what is fair game. We lack any sense of proportion. We often handle such stories so clumsily it is no surprise when the politicians react angrily. Nor is it a surprise when voters are puzzled about what they're supposed to think about what they've just read in their newspapers or seen on the evening news with Tom Brokaw.

The standards of the press have changed along with those of other institutions in our culture. When I started covering politics in the 1950s, we used opaque code words if we found it impossible to avoid discussing some bad behavior by a public official. The late Warren Weaver, Jr., of *The New York Times,* one of the finest newspaper writers of our time, was a master of the euphemism in the days we both were covering the state legislature in Albany. A state senator with a serious drinking problem was described in the *Times* as given to "sometimes excessive conviviality." An assemblyman with a well-established reputation as a womanizer was said to have "an eye for a well-turned ankle."

Now, in the space of a career, we have come to Bill Clinton and Monica Lewinsky on the evening news. Ye gods, Mildred, come listen to this. The president has been having oral sex with some college girl, and right next to the Oval Office, can you believe it!

Some of the stories about the personal lives of presidents and candidates are obviously justified. If the reporters who claim now to have known about John F. Kennedy's peccadilloes had known that one of them involved the girlfriend of a leading Mafia figure, there would have been a political holocaust. The hazards in a president sharing Judith Exner Campbell with Sam Giancana are clear and enormous. That would have been a story about national security, not just philandering.

Similarly, the news media cannot be faulted in any serious way for the attention paid to Senator Edward M. Kennedy's accident at Chappaquiddick in 1969. Although the press mob seemed out of control at times, a young woman had died when that automobile went off the Dike Road into those dark waters. And Kennedy clearly had handled the crisis in a way that suggested, fairly or not, that he was more interested in saving his own skin than in saving Mary Jo Kopechne. His own statement to the voters of Massachusetts that he gave way to "panic, confusion, and doubt" was enough to raise an enduring barrier to winning the presidency, as he discovered when he tried in 1980.

Not all of our politicians' personal lapses are serious, however. On many occasions it is our preoccupation with the trivial that can have serious consequences, particularly when it occurs in a presidential campaign. It can determine who occupies the White House. And although we have learned that the republic can survive second-rate or, lately, even third-rate presidents, it's better not to have the choice result from some press obsession with a tangential question. It's better not to have presidents who are the result of political accidents.

When I began covering politics, the rule was that personal behavior of a public official was fair game only if it might affect his public performance or put the nation at some risk or both. The concern about homosexuality centered on, for example, the possibility of a

White House adviser, State Department official, or member of a key Senate committee being vulnerable to blackmail by some foreign enemy or, for that matter, some American seeking favors.

The same concern, although perhaps far less pressing in the minds of often less than saintly reporters, was that notorious womanizers could be caught in the kind of circumstances that would make them subject to blackmail or irresistible pressure from those trying to influence important decisions. It is not hard to imagine how the nation would react to a president sleeping with a Mafia-connected mistress. But forty years ago any extramarital relationship could be political poison, as Nelson Rockefeller discovered in 1964 when he divorced his first wife and remarried, only to find himself unacceptable to Republican-primary voters and thus forced to admit in the end—it took more than a decade to sink in—that his dreams of the White House could not be fulfilled.

Other politicians of the same era had survived divorce—Adlai Stevenson is the best example—and some, such as Lyndon Johnson, got away with pervasive tales of womanizing that were widely suspected but never proven at the time. But Rockefeller was a Republican seeking support from other Republicans for a presidential nomination. And Republicans were, publicly at least, more socially conservative.

More to the point, Rockefeller was a very different politician because of the wealth and personal celebrity he brought to his late-in-life political calling. So, by divorcing Mary Todhunter Rockefeller after thirty years and marrying Margaretta "Happy" Murphy once she received her contentious divorce to make it possible, Nelson Rockefeller seemed to be flouting the social conventions that applied to most people. And if Republicans in southern Indiana or downstate Illinois were not immediately offended, the sensational press attention given to the story soon pointed the way.

The most celebrated cases of sexual conduct changing the direction of American politics in the last generation were those involving Gary Hart in 1987 and President Bill Clinton a decade later. Hart's fling with Donna Rice cost him the 1988 Democratic presidential nomination and quite possibly the election. Clinton's affair with Monica

Lewinsky led to his impeachment and made a travesty of his second term, when so much had been expected of him.

There were clear similarities between the two episodes. Both Hart and Clinton had established reputations throughout the political community as men with a lively interest in women other than their wives. In Hart's case, it went back to his days as the campaign manager for George McGovern in 1972. So much so that when Hart, embarking on his own campaign in 1983, asked an old ally to round up those volunteers who had been involved in the McGovern campaign in New Hampshire, the friend replied: "You want everybody or just the ones you fucked?"

Clinton's reputation was equally well established in the political world. We all heard stories about him putting a move on a leggy dinner partner or, in one case, the twenty-something daughter of a key political supporter. Attractive wives of some congressional candidates reported he was just a little too enthusiastic when he put his arm around them to pose for a picture. Nobody who knew much about him believed his original denial of the affair with Gennifer Flowers, which he later admitted to, was a lie. No one who knew him misjudged the purpose of the telephone calls he made to Kathleen Willey after spotting her at a campaign rally in Richmond. The "bimbo eruptions" were not just fantasies.

The critical question in both cases, however, was whether the episodes were worth the press attention they were given—and whether the voters were told what they were entitled to know in a balanced form. Hart was furious at the press in 1987, and both Bill and Hillary Rodham Clinton were clearly aggrieved at what they considered unwarranted coverage. The partisans of both candidates argued vehemently that, first, they were being singled out for offenses of which many politicians have been guilty and, second, that their private conduct was essentially irrelevant to their qualifications for the office Hart was seeking and Clinton held.

Their apologists could hardly argue, nonetheless, that either Hart or Clinton behaved in a way that fit the norms for presidential candidates or presidents of the United States or Leaders of the Free World or

whatever. Nor could they argue that Hart and Clinton set a good example for the young and perhaps innocent who believed in the sanc-
tity of marriage. Other presidents who have transgressed have done so
with enough discretion that the press lacked the evidence it needed to
confirm the story. The photo of Hart and Donna Rice on the *Monkey
Business* was such evidence. In Clinton's case, Monica Lewinsky's
taped confessions to Linda Tripp were enough. And Tripp quite aside,
there were many ranking members of the White House staff who
knew something fishy was going on between the boss and the intern,
if not all the lurid details produced by special prosecutor Kenneth Starr
and the witch-hunting Republican partisans who pressed the impeachment case. Some of those staff members remained silent lest they
find themselves subpoenaed by the Republicans and suddenly liable for
huge legal bills.

Hart probably had a legitimate complaint, however, about the feeding frenzy that followed the initial disclosures in *The Miami Herald*
about his time with Donna Rice. Once he admitted to the trip to Bimini and her subsequent weekend visit to his townhouse on Capitol
Hill, the rest was just detail to satisfy the readers' or viewers' appetite
for prurience. But a story like this takes on a life of its own. Reporters
all feel pressure to cut out their own small piece of the action, which
can lead to bizarre quests for new "information" that tells us nothing
we didn't already know—or, at the least, surmise. And the refusal on
the part of the politician to come clean is a goad to many sanctimonious reporters who like to blather on about their duty to "people's
right to know," a phrase never precisely defined.

After the original disclosure of Donna Rice's fateful weekend in
Washington and Hart's denial that it had been anything but an innocent occasion, at least in carnal terms, the candidate tried to resume his
quest for the presidential nomination. He gave a speech in New Jersey
and another at the annual convention of the American Newspaper
Publishers Association in New York. In each case he was mobbed by
reporters and television camera crews demanding more details and
challenging his denials, which were almost impossible for anyone who
had passed puberty to believe.

And as is so often the case in such situations, Hart was faced with trying to explain away inconsistencies in his account of what happened. For example, the candidate's cover story had been that the *Monkey Business* was forced to remain overnight in Bimini because the Customs Office had closed in the late afternoon, before they were planning to leave. But Customs officials, almost predictably, told reporters there was no need for the Hart party to pass through Customs. So, the thinking in the press corps went, if he lied about this, can we believe he and Donna Rice really slept in separate beds? Like hell.

In the end, Hart tried to put out the fire with a press conference in Hanover, New Hampshire, where he was given a public grilling on his personal life that went far beyond anything veteran political reporters, myself included, had ever seen.

Paul Taylor, a well-respected reporter for *The Washington Post,* conducted this interrogation:

Q: Senator, in your remarks yesterday, you raised the issue of morality and you raised the issue of truthfulness. Let me ask you what you mean when you talk about morality and let me be very specific. I have a series of questions about it. When you said you did nothing immoral, did you mean that you had no sexual relationships with Donna Rice last weekend or at any other time you were with her?

A: That is correct, that's correct.

Q: Do you believe that adultery is immoral?

A: Yes.

Q: Have you ever committed adultery?

A: Ahh . . . I do not think that's a fair question.

Q: Well, it seems to me that the question of morality—

A: You can get into some very fine definitions—

Q: —was introduced by you.

A: That's right, that's right.

Q: And it's incumbent upon us to know what your definition of morality is.

A: Well, it includes adultery.

Q: So you believe adultery is immoral?

A: Yes, I do.

Q: Have you ever committed adultery?

A: I do not know—I'm not going into a theological definition of what constitutes adultery. In some people's minds it's people being married and having relationships with other people, so—

Q: Can I ask you whether you and your wife have an understanding about whether or not you can have relationships, you can have sexual encounters with—

A: My inclination is to say, no, you can't ask that question, but the answer is, no, we don't have any such understanding. We have an understanding of faithfulness, fidelity, and loyalty.

Another reporter then asked Hart if his marriage had been "monogamous" except when he and his wife, Lee, were separated. "I do not need to answer that question," Hart replied.

I always considered Paul Taylor an excellent reporter, but I disagreed with the basic premise of his questions because the answers wouldn't tell us anything either we or our readers needed to know or were entitled to know. He was trying to find out whether Gary Hart and Donna Rice had indulged in sexual intercourse on one or both of those weekends. But that wasn't the story. The story was Hart's gross lack of judgment in thinking he could consort with a young woman so openly while trying to maintain his bona fides as the leading candidate for the Democratic nomination for president of the United States.

Did he really believe Americans would elect someone so publicly contemptuous of prevailing standards of behavior? Whether they actually had sex or not wasn't relevant; the failure by Hart was the same either way. And how much did we need to know? If Hart had admitted to sexual congress, would the next question be whether they used the missionary position?

Later that same night the final nail was driven into Hart's political coffin. Taylor called Kevin Sweeney, Hart's press secretary, with the coup de grace. The *Post* had been given conclusive evidence—from a private detective hired to trail Hart by the suspicious husband of another woman—proving that he had been conducting a long-standing affair with another woman who lived in Washington and was known to many in the political community. They had pictures of Hart going into and out of her home, and the woman, through an intermediary, had admitted to the relationship. The *Post* didn't intend to publish her name, but Taylor wanted to question Hart about the story. The ethic of American newspapering requires that the victim be given a chance to reply.

Instead of confirming or denying, the candidate flew back home to Denver and, a few days later, packed it in with an angry press conference in which he combined self-justification with attacks on the news media. It was so strident and unrealistic it reminded many of the older reporters in the room of Richard M. Nixon's "last press conference" after he had lost the 1962 gubernatorial election in California. It apparently reminded Nixon of the same thing. Shortly after Hart pulled out, the disgraced former president wrote him a letter praising him for standing up to the press. It was not a valuable credential for Hart when he tried to make a comeback to the campaign seven months later by filing for the New Hampshire primary shortly before the deadline. His new candidacy caused a brief stir but found few takers.

The Clinton case was quite similar in one respect. Like Hart before him, he seemed to feel he could get away with things that others would be criticized for doing. It was one thing to have a reputation as a womanizer in the past and quite another to have oral sex performed on you by a young intern in a bathroom off the Oval Office. And it was distinctly another thing when he lied about it not only to his staff and supporters but in a deposition that gave an opening to a special prosecutor already trying to bury him—and, not incidentally, to a Republican majority in Congress determined to bring him down at any cost.

Although the Clintons complained about the press and some of their supporters agreed, many others of rank in the administration and the Democratic Party were appalled by his behavior. Bill Clinton was the ultimate user in a milieu in which people are always using one another. How else could anyone view the spectacle of Secretary of State

Madeleine Albright and Secretary of Commerce William Daley, one of the truly savvy ones, standing in the White House driveway and telling the cameras they believed his denials of having sex with "that woman, Miss Lewinsky"?

Like Hart, Clinton had forgotten that he didn't get to be president of the United States single-handedly. A campaign to elect a president necessarily involves many people who put their own lives on a side track to help the candidate, and thus are owed a debt of loyalty. But for Clinton, loyalty ran only one way, from the bottom up. And that is why, although he was acquitted by the Senate in the impeachment trial, he was never cleared in the eyes of many of his fellow Democrats as well as the Republicans. Those Democrats recognized the Republican partisanship driving the whole case and responded in kind to prevent his conviction. If they had been free to vote their opinion without the fear of surrendering the White House, you have to wonder if they would have found him guiltless.

For the nation, the real loss was a second term that could have been fruitful. Because he would no longer have to concern himself with winning reelection, Clinton could have used some of the popularity that helped him defeat Bob Dole in 1996 to tackle the most serious problems facing the nation at the time—most notably, the long-term soundness of the Social Security and Medicare programs. It is something that will never be achieved without some political costs that only a lame-duck president could be expected to absorb. It is possible, of course, that Clinton would have lacked the will to carry it out even without the Lewinsky affair. His most pronounced weakness was that he always wanted everyone to like him. But once he began those liaisons and late-night phone calls to his giggling girlfriend, nothing substantial could be done.

The issue with drinking was never as complicated as those raised by sexual misconduct. It was simply the fear they would be caught drunk when a crisis arose.

The problem for reporters has always been deciding when the rule requires you to write the story and when it makes it possible, if not necessarily responsible, to let it pass. It is rarely easy to see how a politician's private behavior might affect his public performance. And because the consequences of disclosure might be so cataclysmic for the politician, there are precious few cases where that threshold is crossed. Over the years, we political reporters have known about a lot of drunks and lechers but rarely thought their conduct had reached the point of posing a threat to the state or nation. After all, how much harm can a senator do? Heaven knows there have been plenty of drunks reeling around the Senate after lunch, and a few who've been into the vodka before turning up at committee hearings at ten o'clock in the morning.

But there is no evidence that the country suffered from the sometimes impressive drinking by Senator Russell Long of Louisiana, chairman of the powerful Senate Finance Committee. And for Representative Wilbur Mills, chairman of the House Ways and Means Committee, drinking became a public issue only after he started running around with a stripper named Fanne Fox and, one fateful night, drove the two of them into the Tidal Basin off the Potomac near the Jefferson Memorial.

(That one spawned one of the classic good news–bad news jokes of politics after Mills's staff explained lamely that Mrs. Mills hadn't been socializing with her husband and Ms. Fox that night because she was confined to their apartment with a broken foot. The story went that a Mills assistant went to his wife at one in the morning and said, "Mrs. Mills, I have some good news and some bad news. The good news is that your husband was out drinking with a stripper named Fanne Fox and drove his car into the Tidal Basin and a camera crew caught it all on film for the late news on Channel Seven."

"That's the good news?" she asked. "My heavens, what's the bad news?"

"I have to break your foot.")

Editors, too, are wary of stories about the private lives of politicians. I was working for the Gannett Newspapers in their Washington bureau in the early 1960s when it became increasingly apparent that Senator Harrison A. "Pete" Williams, a New Jersey Democrat, was drinking heavily on the job. The topic held some special interest to us because two cities Williams represented, Plainfield and Camden, were also the home bases for Gannett papers. Their readers and Williams's constituents, we thought, were entitled to that information.

But how we were going to handle the story was a problem. You cannot simply accuse a United States senator of being drunk on duty. How could you prove it? Breathalyzer tests are not routinely administered at public hearings of Senate committees. But several of us, observing Williams at such meetings, were convinced he was in the bag. We also knew he made a habit of hanging out at the downtown Gaslight Club, where the beverage of choice was not a chocolate shake. But again, so what?

Finally we were handed what newspapermen call a "peg" for the story after Williams appeared at a dinner meeting of a local Jersey chapter of the NAACP. After the event the group passed a resolution chastising him for his "behavior" without specifying what it found objectionable. We found out he had shown up for the gathering after apparently drinking heavily enough for his condition to be clear to everyone.

We put the story together with care, taking pains with every word and every phrase but nonetheless making it clear for the first time in public that this senator had a drinking problem. Then we put the story on the wire, which relayed our material to Gannett newpapers around the country. One of the two in New Jersey, however, chose not to publish it. They simply didn't have the nerve. When I called the editor to see what had happened, I got a long song and dance about how careful one had to be with such a serious accusation, as if that thought had not occurred to us.

It was a classic case of a news organization letting down its readers by failing to let them in on a little secret known to half of Washington. No one bothered to think about whether the voters of New Jersey might be entitled to know about Pete Williams, and whether that knowledge might make them more interested in whether he should be reelected.

In this case, the editor added insult to injury a few days later. The northern New Jersey reporter for *The New York Times* heard about Williams, and the *Times* carried a page one story, which was then quoted by the Associated Press and distributed to its client papers. Our timid editor now printed the AP story quoting the *Times,* apparently feeling news is better if it marinates for a few days. Another giant of journalism.

There have been times when another personal dimension, the health of the politician, can be the story. Incumbents sometimes will go to great lengths to conceal an illness that might raise questions about their ability to serve. So political reporters are always alert to signs of symptoms such as the back condition, not related to Judith Exner, that plagued John F. Kennedy in the White House. Although medical authorities today may have a different view, there was no reason at the time to suspect that the president's condition or the medications he was taking affected his performance in office. But given their control of the nuclear arsenal, presidents simply are not entitled to total privacy about their health.

These stories are not always of monumental importance, but they do pass on information voters are entitled to have to make a decision on whether a candidate can serve. I encountered my first such case when I was a green reporter for the Rochester, New York, *Times-Union* in the 1950s. It involved a state senator named George Manning who was running for reelection and considered a shoo-in. The paper paid little attention to these contests for legislative seats or minor local offices. Every day we carried short reports on each candidate, with perhaps a small picture of the incumbent or challenger. The picture we were using of Manning was several years old and showed him as the exemplar of good health, if perhaps a little heavy in the jowls. But then someone told me that he had not shown up for meetings at which the paper had reported him giving a brief talk. Instead, someone on his staff read the statement and made his apologies. A few telephone calls confirmed it had become a pattern.

We soon learned that Manning was in the late stages of an undetermined illness and had lost so much weight he looked nothing like the picture we were using. When I asked his chief aide about his health, she told me it was none of my business. And when I tried to insist on seeing him, she told me the same thing in somewhat stronger terms, particularly for a genteel, middle-aged woman in that era. We finally tracked him down and learned he had an unforgiving form of cancer. In those days cancer was considered by some people to be a scandal rather than a misfortune, but we couldn't confirm the diagnosis and carry a story about it. So we settled for sending a photographer to get a new photo, in which he appeared skeletal. The voters paid little attention and reelected him to another term, but he died before he could return to Albany.

At the level of presidential politics, the personal life of the candidate is a much more important story, even when the story is false and based on the inability of the mainstream press to avoid joining the bottom-feeders.

There is a sorry pattern in the way these stories develop. First, those of us in the mainstream press hear that somebody else—meaning some competitor—is about to break a story that will "blow the roof off" the campaign. Often the "somebody else" is supposed to be a reporter or columnist for some out-of-Washington newspaper, so we are faced with the ultimate shame of being beaten by someone who doesn't even cover the campaign. After the rumors, sometimes concocted by political enemies of the candidate being targeted, have circulated for a few days or perhaps a couple of weeks, someone finally publishes or broadcasts a "story" about the gossip that has been making the rounds.

Then it becomes a question of what the responsible news outlets do with it. If they ignore it, they tell themselves, they are denying their readers or viewers information that "everybody" already knows. "It's out there," goes the rationale. On the other hand, we know that this story, if true, would be both significant and extremely damaging to someone. And finally, it seems inevitably, these stories creep into the mainstream media, and some of them cause great harm and persist for years.

Some editors and television-news executives handle salacious stories about public figures in the guise of exposing how the story ever came out in the first place and then examining the ethics of those who have used the material. Tut-tut.

That was the way ABC News handled the story of Gennifer Flowers, Governor Bill Clinton's sometime girlfriend, after it appeared in a supermarket tabloid, the *Star*. ABC originally ignored the disclosure, then scheduled a *Nightline* program to discuss the ethical questions confronting the press. The panelists included a media critic for *Newsweek* (Jonathan Alter), a political science professor (Larry Sabato) who had written a book called *Feeding Frenzy* about press behavior in these situations, and someone from the Clinton campaign. The "someone" was Mandy Grunwald, a young media consultant to the campaign who proved to be very bad news for the usually unflappable Ted Koppel. Not to put too fine a point on it, she ate his lunch.

The *Nightline* host, in his full cluck-clucking mode, asked her if a story like this could "develop a sort of momentum of its own."

> GRUNWALD: Well, programs like this are not a help, Ted. This is the first program that *Nightline* has done on any topic relating to the Democratic presidential primaries. You haven't been talking about the middle class. You haven't talked about why Bill Clinton has captured people's imagination. Here you are—
>
> KOPPEL: Oh, now, now wait a second. Wait a second. You're making a charge that's not accurate. We've done a number of programs on the middle class. We've done a number of programs on—
>
> GRUNWALD: You have not.
>
> KOPPEL: —the issues, unemployment. You're quite right. We haven't done a program on Bill Clinton.
>
> GRUNWALD: But here we are just a couple of weeks before the New Hampshire primary. People are about to go out there and vote. . . . They have real concerns. And you're choosing with your editorial comment, by making this program about some unsubstantiated charges that . . . started with a trashy supermarket tabloid. You're telling people that something you think is important. That's not context. You're setting the agenda and you're letting the *Star* set it for you.

It was a scolding that delighted many viewers of *Nightline* who found Ted Koppel sometimes a tad sanctimonious. And here he was, of all people, purveying a salacious story under the pretext of a sober discussion of the ethics of the news business. The ratings for the program were unquestionably enhanced by the juicy subject matter, and no viewer could complain it was dull.

In the long run, no one could claim that Clinton had been mistreated. The tabloid story of his sexual relationship with Flowers was, he admitted, true. But many of the scandal stories the press handles or mishandles are both false and damaging.

One victim of both rumor and guilt by association was Jack Kemp, the former Buffalo Bills quarterback who later served in Congress and the Bush cabinet and eventually became the Republican nominee for vice president in 1996. This story went back to 1967 when Kemp, a Californian, was serving in an off-season job in Sacramento on the staff of Governor Ronald Reagan, for whom he had campaigned in the 1966 election in which Reagan defeated Democratic Governor Edmund G. "Pat" Brown. Someone uncovered the shocking news that Reagan's chief of staff was a homosexual who headed a "homo ring" that had been holding "homo parties" at a ski lodge he owned in Lake Tahoe, Nevada.

Kemp's crime was that he had bought a share of the ski lodge as an investment. But he had never been to the lodge or joined any of the parties; he was looking for a sound way to make a profit in real estate. And Kemp was, by every testimonial, a very heterosexual male, which was particularly important in the Republican Party of that day and is still an absolute requirement of the fundamentalist Christian wing of the party today.

The story kept coming up, however, year after year. Sometimes the canard was debunked by sympathetic writers, such as columnists Rowland Evans and Robert D. Novak, or by magazine writers who had conducted extensive inquiries and found no evidence Kemp was gay. These pieces would go on at length about how unfair it was that this issue was still being raised against good old Jack Kemp. But the effect was to keep the rumor "out there" for another generation of readers and to provide an excuse for other news organizations to go over the same ground, reach the same conclusion, and, of course, keep the "story" alive. NBC's *Today* show, for example, did a piece that then was picked up by the Associated Press and distributed to hundreds of newspapers. The bottom line was that there were all these false rumors about Jack Kemp and wasn't that terrible, folks. But some people are going to suspect fire when they see smoke, so all the rationalizations about doing Kemp a favor rang a little hollow.

One major result was that Kemp's attempt to seek the Republican nomination for president in 1988 was stunted from the outset. Contributors and potential supporters in such key primary states as New Hampshire shied away from the old quarterback, fearing they would be embarrassed for having backed the wrong horse if "the story came out." The fact that there was no story seemed beside the point.

Kemp probably wouldn't have won the nomination anyway. The leading candidates that year were then Vice President George Bush and Senate Republican leader Bob Dole, and they took up most of the attention of a press corps that usually cannot cover more than two candidates and chew gum at the same time. In any case, for some of the social conservatives Kemp was too serious about broadening the base of the Republican Party by bringing more black people into the tent. He also had a tendency to deliver endless speeches covering every topic on the national agenda. Even Republicans who admired him said in 1988 that Bush would never choose him for vice president because, as the late Barber Conable, a congressman from New York, told me at the time, "George would have visions of Jack arriving for their weekly lunch in the White House with two armloads of manila envelopes full of position papers." But windy or not, he was always burdened by the rumors about the homosexual ring in Sacramento from so long ago.

The elder George Bush had a problem of his own dealing with persistent rumors while he was vice president in 1981, and again when preparing to run for the 1988 nomination six years later. In his case, the story was that he had been involved in a long relationship with a woman other than Barbara Bush. The identity of the woman changed from time to time. Once it was an attractive blond congressional widow who still lived in a Capitol Hill townhouse in Washington.

More often, the story was that it was his longtime de facto chief of staff.

Every news organization with a serious presence in Washington assigned reporters to investigate the situation, and they all came up empty, which did not disprove the allegation but made it one that no responsible newspaper or network was likely to report. The rumors were so virulent, however, that the Bush campaign managers in 1987 decided it was better to confront them rather than have "the story" surface in some quarter that the mainstream press would not ignore. So they arranged for the first son, George W. Bush, to follow the novel course of trying to squelch a rumor by publicly raising it. He was quoted in a brief item in *Newsweek* magazine's "Periscope" column: "The answer to the Big A question is N.O."

The story would not die, however. In October, during the height of the general election campaign, a so-called "alternative paper" on the West Coast, the *L.A. Weekly,* published a report on all the rumors of Bush's affairs without providing any evidence at all. The story originally was easy for the mainstream news operations to ignore; most of them had conducted their own inquiries long before the campaign and found them fruitless.

But these stories always find their way into the general population of the news business. Or, put another way, even the best newspapers get drawn into or trapped by the lowest common denominator. In this case, this little nugget of journalistic enterprise was picked up by two British tabloids—no surprise there—and by the New York *Daily News,* which should have known better. Then a few days later a rumor raced through Wall Street that *The Washington Post* was going to expose Bush's relationship and identify the mistress. The rumor caused a sharp and sudden drop on the stock market, and that economic news became the story—and an excuse to raise the question of the vice president's personal life even though *Post* editors immediately denied there was any such story in the works.

The next day a middle-level political professional on the Dukakis staff, Donna Brazile, added enough fuel to make the story of Bush's private life one that no news organization could ignore. Brazile correctly accused the Bush campaign of using "racist" tactics with the infamous Willie Horton commercial about a black man who had carried out a brutal attack in Maryland while on a weekend furlough from a prison in Massachusetts. But then, talking to reporters who had gathered for the Al Smith dinner in New York, she added: "I think George Bush owes it to the American people to fess up. The American people have every right to know if Barbara Bush will share that bed with him in the White House." Brazile was quickly fired by the straightlaced Dukakis, but the Bush story was "out there" for the last weeks of the campaign.

If there was a killer rumor in the 1988 campaign, however, it was one that began on the extremist-nut fringe and soon found its way into the journalistic mainstream. It started at the Democratic National Convention in Atlanta when followers of Lyndon LaRouche, a crackpot political cultist, passed around flyers claiming that Dukakis had been treated for emotional illness on two occasions, immediately after the death of his brother Stelian in an automobile accident and then after Dukakis lost the 1978 Democratic primary for governor to Edward King, a conservative onetime pro football player whose principal distinction as a candidate was an endorsement from Carl Yastrzemski.

Considering the source—the LaRouche people were the same ones who insisted Queen Elizabeth was a drug pusher—it was easy for reporters covering the campaign to ignore the story. So they laughed off rumors that some gossip columnists for the *Chicago Tribune* or *Detroit News* were planning to "blow the lid off the whole thing." Then, at a press conference in Boston, a reporter for the *Boston Herald* asked Dukakis whether he had ever been treated for emotional illness.

I considered this a breach of ethics by the reporter. Just the fact that the question was asked in a public setting while the television cameras were running meant it had been thrust into the public domain. It had become fodder for all the dingbat radio and cable television shows that did no reporting of their own but instead exploited what they were handed. The proper and decent way for a reporter to proceed in such situations is to confront the politician one-on-one to get an answer, then decide whether the reply is newsworthy and whether to go public with it. The startled Dukakis brushed aside the question, but it was now "out there." So later his campaign press secretary, Dayton Duncan, was obliged to issue a statement saying that Dukakis "has never been treated for mental depression or mental illness of any kind at any time."

The Boston Globe, faced with an awkward competitive situation, reported the question far down in a lengthy story and followed it with a paragraph saying that there was no evidence to support the rumor.

Not everyone was so discreet, however, although many major newspapers—including *The Washington Post* and the Baltimore *Sun,* for whom I worked then—published nothing about it. *The Washington Times* carried a story under the headline DUKAKIS PSYCHIATRIC RUMOR DENIED. And the following day *The New York Times* allowed itself to become a little pregnant by carrying a short story on an inside page under the mealymouthed headline CANDIDATES' HEALTH DISCUSSED.

In the end, however, there was no way to control the "story." Asked by a shouting reporter for comment about Dukakis's refusal to release his medical records, President Reagan replied as the cameras rolled, "I'm not going to pick on an invalid." That tore it. Now it had become a story that all the networks and all newspapers would carry. Presidents are not ignored, even when we don't know if they are simply making an unthinking wisecrack, as Reagan was inclined to do, or trying to make mischief for a political opponent, which he also had been known to do.

In any case, Dukakis was now obliged to arrange for his personal physician to testify at a press conference that the candidate was in "excellent health" and had never experienced any "psychological symptoms, complaints, or treatment." And Reagan felt obliged to call Dukakis and apologize. But the harm was done. Over the next ten days polling for both his campaign and Bush's campaign showed him losing eight percentage points.

The whole "story" had been a total fiction, but enough Americans were gullible enough or suspicious enough of politicians in general to believe there was something fishy going on. They were right. The fishy thing was the press role in the episode. We always seem to find some excuse for feeding on the bottom. And the consequences can be far more serious than we recognize, judging by the cavalier way we sometimes make decisions about what to print or say.

There is no reason to believe that the incident cost Michael Dukakis the White House. There were a half dozen strategic campaign decisions that could be blamed for his defeat, the most significant being his failure to recognize how Bush could use such issues as the flag and Willie Horton to persuade voters he was a better alternative. But a switch of only 4 percent of the vote would have reversed the result. So the episode was not trivial.

The discovery of a skeleton in the closet doesn't always involve the candidate's sex life, drinking habits, or emotional state. Money can be the topic, as it was—on the surface, at least—in the wild press assault in 1984 on Representative Geraldine Ferraro of New York, the Democratic Party's surprise candidate for vice president. It preoccupied the political world and much of the media for two weeks just before Labor Day and robbed Fritz Mondale of any slim hope that he might defeat President Reagan.

The problem began when Ferraro backtracked on her original promise to make public both her own income tax returns and those of her husband, John Zaccaro, a lawyer and real estate operator. He just wasn't willing to surrender his privacy for business reasons, she said, and he was hanging tough. "If you're married to an Italian man, you know what it's like," she explained.

The gumshoes of the Fourth Estate were immediately suspicious. They already had discovered that her 1978 congressional election campaign had been forced to pay a civil fine, a common occurrence in politics but still an irregularity worth running down. And there were essentially technical questions about the accuracy of her filing with the House Ethics Committee in which she appeared to be disclaiming any continuing and thorough knowledge of her husband's affairs. Again, no big deal, but now there was this from her husband. What did John Zaccaro—and Geraldine Ferraro—have to hide?

Underlying all these suspicions was the fact that their names ended in a vowel. Was he "connected"—meaning part of the Mafia—or something like that? No one in the press or political community voiced those suspicions in those terms, but everyone knew that if her name had been Florence Nightingale and his had been John Alden, the inquiries would not have had the same edge.

So Zaccaro-Ferraro was the target of a frenzied effort to find the evidence that must be there on any Italian American, right? It turned out that a minor mob figure had once rented an apartment in a building Zaccaro inherited from his father in 1971 and sold almost immediately. Hmm, very suspicious. And Ferraro's campaign for the House of Representatives had received a contribution of a handsome seven hundred dollars from a man once convicted on a labor racketeering charge. So she claims she didn't know him. That's what they all say.

Worse yet, another intrepid reporter discovered that when her parents ran a neighborhood grocery store in Newburgh, New York, forty years earlier, they had taken bets on numbers. Can you imagine that—selling policy in a neighborhood store! Who ever heard of such a thing?

The one discovery that caused the most heartburn for the Mondale campaign was that Zaccaro had once borrowed $100,000 from the trust of a widow for whom he was a conservator. He had paid the money back with interest, but it was, nonetheless, a violation of the rules that govern lawyers acting in that capacity. So the raised eyebrows were justified, and so was the Mondale campaign's regret about the sloppy job they had done in vetting Zaccaro. But what all that had to do with Ferraro was never made clear. Nor was much attention paid to the much broader question of whether there was any precedent for so much scrutiny of a vice presidential candidate's spouse. Had all of those wives of other nominees been purer than the driven snow? Do we know?

In the end, Ferraro dealt with all of the issues hanging "out there" with a truly remarkable performance at a press conference. After her lawyers and accountants answered questions for a full eighty minutes, the candidate herself answered more of them with poise and high good humor for one hour and fifty minutes. All of it ran on cable television and much of it on the networks, so the political pressure was enormous on this green candidate for the vice presidency, and she received far higher marks than her green-eyeshade inquisitors in the press.

Particularly telling was the reaction in Dallas, where the Republican National Convention had been put on hold for a few hours while everyone watched the press conference. For several days Republicans had been snickering about her troubles and enjoying the speculation about whether she might be dropped from the ticket like Tom Eagleton had been twelve years earlier. So they were relishing the prospect of watching her squirm. Instead, the professionals in the crowd came away impressed, albeit reluctantly, by the way she handled herself under what they recognized was the ultimate political pressure. At lunch an hour later Drew Lewis, a smart pol who had been governor of Pennsylvania and Reagan cabinet secretary, said, "Now there's a vice president who could be president"—a particularly intriguing testimonial to those who knew Lewis as one of the principal champions of George H. W. Bush for Reagan's ticket in 1980.

The detailed exposition of Ferraro's private life showed she had no problem with her income taxes, although their accountants discovered a fifty-thousand-dollar delinquency in John Zaccaro's returns that was paid off with interest. Nor had Ferraro been guilty of a conflict of interest by casting any congressional votes that might have affected their personal holdings. In short, it turned out that John Zaccaro was not a secret Mafia kingpin, and Geraldine Ferraro was another street-smart, tough politician from Queens.

We also learned, sometime after the fact, that Ferraro didn't know much about Zaccaro's handling of their financial affairs. In the daylong session with accountants preparing for the press conference, she discovered that her husband had established two trust funds for their son but only one for each of their two daughters. Others in the room said she turned to her husband and said: "We're going to fix that tomorrow, right, John?"

After it was over, the Mondale campaign was predictably chagrined at its failure to uncover potential problems when they vetted Ferraro and Zaccaro before she was named for the ticket. They complained about how they had lost two weeks of the campaign in which they might have set the agenda and gained momentum. And Ferraro herself was chagrined because, as a professional politician, she knew that the last thing a vice presidential nominee wants to do is make a mistake that hurts the ticket.

In fact, however, it was hard to see what mistake she made. She could hardly be held responsible for reporters running amok because they thought they had discovered the Godfather and his moll.

It was even harder to see that there had ever been much realistic hope that Mondale could defeat Reagan under the best circumstances. Gerry Ferraro was not the only problem he had to overcome. At the same time, Jesse Jackson was still jerking Mondale around. And the Democrat's managers already had screwed up several other aspects of the campaign, making the prospects even dimmer.

The true lesson in Ferraro's candidacy, in that time of crisis and throughout the campaign, was that she was a full-grown politician every bit as well equipped as the men who had occupied the same position. Indeed, she was clearly superior to many of them. It speaks volumes about our sense of values in politics when she is remembered by some more as a controversial figure because of some mix-up about her finances than as the woman who broke the gender barrier for the national ticket in a convincing way.

So the evidence is abundant that the mainstream press is too often led into indefensible behavior by the less responsible elements on the fringes of journalism, if they can be considered part of the craft at all. And the evidence is equally abundant that these unfounded stories can have a significant, perhaps even determinative, effect on American political life up to and including the election of the president of the United States.

Why does it happen? The popular answer is that "they want to sell newspapers" or, in the case of television, "that's what gets the ratings."

That theory is dead wrong about newspapers. It is true, of course, that newspapers need circulation to attract advertising and the income to pay the salaries of their editors and reporters. If their circulation doesn't keep pace with that of competitors, they collapse, a lesson I learned as one of those left on the street when the late, great *Washington Star* went down in 1981. But in more than fifty years in the business, I have never seen coverage of an individual story driven by the need to "sell newspapers." Circulation simply doesn't come up in newsrooms. To those in the trade, the notion is ridiculously naïve. Reporters and editors don't think that way. They think about beating their competitors, and they care—perhaps too much—about the opinions of their peers.

Television is a different dish of tea. The networks and the individual stations need ratings just as newspapers need circulation. But the difference is that news is not the prime product of the networks, not the one that determines whether they succeed or fail. The news directors and correspondents are, however, just as competitive and peer-conscious as their counterparts in newspapers. And they are just as reluctant as newspapermen to carry stories about politicians that are false, unfair, or both.

But the news business in this age is not made up only of the broadcast networks and the mainstream newspapers. The cable networks— CNN, Fox News Channel, MSNBC, CNBC—are heavily dependent on what they call "news." Their normally modest ratings rise sharply when there is a story that attracts almost universal attention and provides great pictures. That can be a war or a hurricane or a presidential election, or it can be Lady Di or O. J. Simpson or Michael Jackson or a political scandal. They need to provide the pictures for those engaged viewers, but more to the point, they need raw material for the talk shows that are almost entirely derivative.

I have little sympathy for most of the purveyors of political wisdom on cable or radio talk shows. They are quick to hand down judgments and short of any basic or original information gleaned from their own reporting. Most of them have never covered a fire. So it is mostly uninformed blather and bitter attacks on the hapless liberals who are usually cannon fodder on those programs. Again, I have the credential of having been part of that process too often.

I have to confess I am also offended by the smug glee shown by the cable and radio wise men as they hand down their verdicts on this politician or that one. Most of them have never done anything, in journalism or any other field, to give their opinions serious weight. Their only credential is that they are holding the microphone. Their only apparent purpose is to be provocative or outlandish enough to attract listeners or viewers who otherwise might be tuning in Jerry Springer.

To all of this, we now have added still another outlet that may have even more potential for mischief: the Internet. It is a medium that can be used by anyone and thus an ideal vehicle for the destructive story that may be false and even ridiculous but inevitably finds its way into the mainstream of news in America. Politicians beware.

11

KEEPING SECRETS
FROM THE VOTERS

*E*ven when we are not being taken over the jumps by trash stories originating in some political storm sewer, those of us who cover politics fall far short of giving readers and viewers what they should know as prospective voters.

We lack candor because we are timid. Reporters and, more often, editors fear that the use of the most direct language about a politician occupying a high office will make us vulnerable to complaints of bias and leave us subject to retaliation. In fact, political writers who have been around the track know those fears are largely unfounded. We recognize, as do the politicians, that these are symbiotic relationships. If we need them, they need us just as much. If a president or a candidate takes a burn and won't give us an interview, we probably haven't lost much. If they are willing to talk to us, it is not because they find us so charming.

Equally important and damning, the press accepts and reinforces images of people and situations that are far from accurate. We fail to tell readers important things that we know about politicians and their world—the so-called "inside" information that might affect their view of elected officials, candidates, and issues.

Our failure of candor applies most obviously to presidents and candidates for president. They are the ones with the muscle, so they are the ones we tiptoe around, unnecessarily in my view.

When, to cite a classic case, George W. Bush was the Republican nominee for president in 2000, there was a broad suspicion in the political community and the political press corps—a suspicion bordering on a consensus—that he was too dumb to be Leader of the Free World. His use of language was often halting, and he seemed to lack some basic knowledge. People who had known him for a while confided that he wasn't too swift, a great guy but not a great student. But of course, no one expressed those doubts in so many words—or at least not in public.

Instead, we danced around the issue, relying on the reader to draw the correct inference. The favored word was *gravitas,* as in: Does Bush have the gravitas to persuade Americans he should be elected to the White House? Or alternatively, when we tired of *gravitas:* Is he too *light* for the office? Does he lack the weight? Or the heft? There were countless ways to imply what we thought without saying it in so many words—and earning the enmity of the Republicans and quite possibly the next president.

There were, to be sure, questions raised in the press about his refusal to release his grades from his prep school and college years in which his classmates' reports suggested he had not distinguished himself academically. In the end, however, no one in the press or in politics is willing to say in so many words, flat out, that someone is too dumb for the office, even if that view is widespread.

Even political opponents are cautious in what they say about a president. Representative Richard Gephardt of Missouri, the former Democratic leader in the House, described for *The Washington Post* editorial board how difficult it was to communicate with Bush about the war in Iraq.

"He just doesn't say anything. I mean I guess he hears me but he didn't say anything. He didn't say yes or no or you're right or you're wrong or maybe or let's talk about [Iraq] or anything. It just goes by. It's like I just arrived from Mars." But even after that burst of candor, Gephardt avoided the judgment that the president was not intellectually equipped for the job. "He's not dumb," he said, "but he is not informed and he's not experienced."

Intellect is not necessarily a requirement for a president. We learned from Jimmy Carter that being the smartest kid on the block doesn't mean a successful presidency. And we learned from Ronald Reagan that a lack of intellectual interests and insight doesn't guarantee a failure in the White House. Being smart isn't everything. Antonin Scalia is obviously very bright, but would you want him in the White House?

And anyway, does it really matter? George W. Bush may not be too swift, but nobody thinks Karl Rove is dumb. This is something the voters have to decide for themselves, but they are entitled to more information than they usually are given on which to base the decision.

As the 2000 campaign progressed, Bush may have even benefited from the doubts about his intellect. Thus, the standard for judging his first debate with Gore was essentially that he was acceptable because he was passably articulate and didn't drool. By contrast, there was the negative story about Gore sighing so conspicuously and thus suggesting an arrogance and petulance the voters do not find either attractive or reassuring. Many Democrats were angry at the press for giving Bush such an easy passing grade, and in retrospect I was inclined to agree with them, although I was one of the guilty parties. On reflection, I suspect both candidates probably deserved to be disparaged.

But reporters have a problem when they avoid being direct and blunt in their language and rely on the voters to draw the correct inferences from oblique approaches, such as the whole question about whether someone has enough gravitas. The vast majority of those readers who will understand what we are trying to say are also the ones who don't need to be told. They figured that out for themselves long ago. The problem is that we in the press fancy ourselves dealing with facts that can be proven to be facts. If we are going to say that anyone— let alone a president—is dumb, we need some hard evidence that is rarely available.

So the bottom line is that if the voters are interested in how smart a candidate for president may be, they have to figure it out for themselves. Some of the election returns indicate there may not be enough information for them to do so.

Another enormous problem for the press is how to deal with a political leader or president who is lying. We are afraid to call them "liars" or to say they are telling "lies." But it happens often, even with presidents, you may be shocked to discover. So we are reduced to all sorts of substitute words and phrases. We say they are guilty of "misstatements" or "statements not supported by the evidence." We say they "misspoke" or "stretched the truth" or even that they "played fast and loose with the truth" or "strained our credulity." In extremis, we accuse them of "misrepresenting the facts," suggesting that it was purposefully done.

My favorite device was to quote a politician caught in an obvious lie and add that he said it "with a straight face." I once tried to get by with a line about a politician "whose nose appeared to be growing as he spoke," but a literal-minded editor wisely spiked that one.

So we didn't say President Bush lied in his justification for the attack on Iraq, although the facts pointed that way. There were no weapons of mass destruction and no evidence of a tie between Iraq and Osama bin Laden or Al Qaeda. Nor were the Iraqis a threat to the United States, as the president, Vice President Dick Cheney, and all their hired hands kept insisting. Those were all lies we didn't label as such. Some of the comedians on late-night television called them that, and the editorial cartoonists who appear in our own newspapers don't mince words. Nor do some of the blowhards on talk radio, cable television, and the Internet. They may be wrong on the facts or egregiously fatheaded, but they don't lack candor.

By contrast, the problem for the mainstream press covering politics—meaning largely newspapers and the broadcast-television networks—is the requirement that we prove what we say is true. How do we know the president is lying? Maybe he did misspeak. How do we know what the president knows that we don't know? He may have something up his sleeve. So we make statements like "The president has been guilty of 'misstatements'" and expect the reader or viewer to translate that into "lies."

But it doesn't work. When Bush finally admitted on September 17, 2003, two years after the fact, that there was "no evidence" connecting Saddam Hussein and Iraq to the September 11 terrorist assaults on the World Trade Center and the Pentagon, it was too late. Opinion surveys showed many Americans, a majority in some studies, believed there was such an Iraq–Al Qaeda connection. And the story about his admission of error received modest play. In other words, Bush got away with it. But you have to wonder if he would have escaped responsibility so easily if the press had been more direct in its coverage instead of pussyfooting for two years.

In some cases, it doesn't seem to matter if they are telling lies. When a question arose as to whether Ronald Reagan had signed a critical document in the Iran-Contra affair, many of us assumed that he had done so and simply forgotten. In fact, a couple of weeks after I offered that theory only half facetiously on a television program, I ran into a White House adviser who told me, "You were closer than you knew."

In the case of Bill Clinton and Monica Lewinsky, his denials were so patently insincere, nobody believed them. The conventional wisdom, right again, held that everybody lies about sex. The Democrats in the Senate didn't vote against impeachment because they believed Clinton; they voted to acquit him as a reaction to a clearly partisan impeachment by the Republicans.

In dealing with presidents, there is a factor other than the normal sensitivity to criticism among editors that reinforces whatever tendency we have to soften our language. Even though we know the people who occupy the office to be ordinary people, the office itself commands a respect it is impossible to ignore. That is the case even with old hands in Washington who reflect the national ethic.

Most Americans tend to view any president with awe, a mistake in every case I have experienced but nonetheless true. If you look at the pictures, everyone who meets a president seems to be smiling, whatever feelings they may be hiding. So if the political reporter is too blunt in language or manner, there is often a public reaction. On more than one occasion I received letters or telephone calls from viewers chastising me for referring on television to "Reagan" or "Clinton" without using the title. When my partner, Jules Witcover, and I wrote columns for the *Washington Star* about how Reagan didn't have his facts right at a press conference, we received letters telling us not to be such nitpickers. He wasn't called "the Teflon president" for nothing.

Many old pols share a similar regard for the niceties of the business. The late Thomas P. "Tip" O'Neill, the longtime Speaker of the House of Representatives, always referred publicly to every president, even those he held in minimum high regard, as "the president of the United States." The full title, nothing less.

The problem of candor in politics is less difficult when dealing with politicians other than the president. The aura around them is obviously less mystical, and they are rarely surrounded by the legions of sycophants in every White House. Most of the good ones, moreover, have objective minds and understand that there is usually nothing personal in a tough question from a reporter.

We are often accused of going easy on a politician because we fear losing access, but that is a fanciful notion held largely by conspiracy theorists who don't know how news coverage works. The politicians and reporters both know that if we don't get the information from one source, we will probably get it somewhere else. There is always some disgruntled staff member or a bitter rival or a jealous colleague. And if the politician won't deal with me today, he will probably change his mind tomorrow when the facts of a story may put him in a more favorable light.

Perhaps a failure of the press more serious than its inability to call a liar a liar is our willingness to accept and adopt perceptions of both people and situations that are not accurate. And to the extent that that happens, potential voters are denied information they might wish to consider. The problem is simply that we don't tell what we—meaning everyone in the political world—all know.

Sometimes we simply pass on mistaken perceptions. The reputation of the late Lee Atwater is an example. When Atwater was serving as chairman of the Republican National Committee early in the first Bush administration, he was diagnosed with a brain cancer that put him out of action, at least temporarily, and soon threatened his life. So the Republicans designated Charles Black, a veteran consultant and Atwater's onetime business partner, the chairman's temporary spokesman. He was widely described on television and in some newspapers as Atwater's "protégé."

To anyone who knew the people involved, this was preposterous on its face. The truth was the reverse. Atwater, like several others of his generation, had been a protégé of Charlie Black in the ranks of young conservative Republican campaign operatives. But most people in the press didn't know Black, and they accepted the image that had been created of Atwater as a political genius because he had successfully managed George H. W. Bush's triumph over Michael Dukakis in the 1988 election. And Charlie went along with the gag, offering a wry smile when some uninformed reporter asked him about how his "mentor" Atwater was coming along.

I knew Atwater throughout his career in politics, starting when he was an acolyte of Strom Thurmond in South Carolina, and I enjoyed him immensely. He was great company at dinner, pausing over his storytelling only to lavish Tabasco sauce on every dish. He loved the intrigue of politics and was fascinated by tales of who did what to whom. But his reputation as a political genius was greatly inflated. He was a master at telling reporters about some situation in a way that reflected well on himself and not so well on others but without leaving any visible fingerprints. I particularly recall him describing how difficult it was to persuade Bush to do some of the harsh things he did to his New Hampshire primary opponent Bob Dole in the 1988 campaign. It turned out that John Sununu, the governor of New Hampshire and later Bush's chief of staff, was the one who had insisted. And yes, when you got right down to it, Bush finally agreed.

Atwater was not as much a master of politics as he was a master of spin. He knew the Cotton South well, and he was quick to recognize weaknesses in the opposition that provided tactical opportunities for his own candidates. Beginning in 1985, he also knew the steps to take to give Bush some access to southern conservative Republicans. So the credit he was given for Bush's success in 1988 was probably justified, at least in part—although, of course, if Dukakis had not been such an inept candidate, we might never have heard of Lee Atwater again.

Atwater's reputation in the business was as a political hired gun who had no reservations about using the harshest negative tactics. In South Carolina he had gained renown among politicians for "going negative" with a vengeance in behalf of clients such as Representative (and later Governor) Carroll Campbell. In one infamous case he described a rival who had been treated in a hospital for emotional illness when he was young as having been "hooked up to jumper cables."

From his deathbed Atwater apologized to that rival, a lawyer and populist political activist named Tom Turnipseed. He also apologized to a Republican colleague at the eleventh hour for lying to him about the role he had played in staging a fake protest against Ronald Reagan by a particularly scruffy group in the hope of evoking a backlash against the Democrats and sympathy for Reagan. When NBC carried a story about Atwater's "dirty trick," he had denied it inside the campaign, moving the press officer to chastise the NBC reporter even to the point of denying her access to anyone in the campaign. Only much later did he discover that Atwater had boasted of his role to the young woman who shared an apartment with the NBC reporter.

Lee Atwater was not Saddam Hussein, of course. He was a southern boy with no little charm and a streak of meanness who wanted to win elections at any cost. That is not the way he was perceived by the press—or by the voters who cared, if any. Instead, on the strength of his part in the 1988 campaign, he became a major celebrity, at least by Washington standards.

That kind of thing happens all the time. James Carville jokes about all the years he spent laboring on obscure and mostly losing campaigns before he became an "instant" genius showing the way for Bill Clinton in the presidential campaign of 1992. From that point on, Democratic candidates were falling all over themselves to get Carville's services. At a minimum he would be a credential signifying to potential contributors and voters that this one was a serious campaign.

Carville was being solicited for his opinion on a whole panoply of political questions and flooded with high-dollar speaking engagements from lecture agents. Everybody loves a winner.

Once someone becomes a celebrity, one way or another, it clings. A month or two after resigning the vice presidency in disgrace and admitting his corruption in a nolo contendere plea that kept him out of jail, Spiro Agnew was applauded when he walked through downtown Washington restaurants. It doesn't matter what you've done as long as it gets you on television.

Not all of those with inflated or distorted reputations have been Republicans, of course. One classic case of a Democrat never seen very clearly by the press or voters was then Senator Eugene J. McCarthy of Minnesota, the liberal hero who led the campaign in 1968 to unseat President Lyndon B. Johnson because of his conduct of the Vietnam War.

Challenging a president of your own party, and particularly one as tough as Johnson—"He'll burn your barn," they used to say—was a gritty political act. McCarthy was not part of the so-called "inner club" of the Senate—he wrote poetry in his spare time, for heaven's sake—but he was generally accepted within the party and popular enough back home to be assured of a long career at the highest levels of national politics, a career he obviously put at risk when he filed against Johnson in the New Hampshire primary.

His candidacy, he said at the outset, was less about winning the presidency than about forcing a change in the policy that was killing so many young Americans in Southeast Asia. He was to be a vehicle for change, he told us. In some ways he was the ideal man for the moment—intellectual, professorial, both witty and articulate as well as principled. His avowed purity of purpose struck a chord with the young people always seeking idealism and in 1968 bound together in their anger about the war. So it was no surprise when thousands of college students swarmed into New Hampshire to help. Declaring themselves "Clean for Gene," they shaved their beards and washed their faces and did their drugs, if any, in the most inconspicuous way.

It paid off when McCarthy captured 42 percent of the vote,

enough to make him the de facto winner against a sitting president who managed 49 percent.

The young legions stuck with their hero, moreover, after Johnson, facing outright defeat at McCarthy's hands in Wisconsin, withdrew from the field and Senator Robert F. Kennedy announced his candidacy and became, in the eyes of the political world and the press, the heavyweight challenger for the nomination. With those who were Clean for Gene, Kennedy was an opportunist who had not been prepared to risk his career when it seemed like more of a long-odds bet. More than any other factor, their devotion to their hero was a measure of their idealism and hope.

But as the campaign progressed, McCarthy began to change in subtle ways. He was understandably irked by Kennedy's entry into the competition, although he already had accomplished his original stated purpose by driving Johnson to the sidelines. He became waspish about his new rival, and miffed at the press reports on the huge throngs that were surrounding Kennedy, tearing at his cuff links and tugging at his sleeves in a frenzy reflecting his special place as the younger brother of the fallen President John F. Kennedy. The reaction was as intense and frenetic as any of those covering the campaign had seen in American politics, so the stories were legitimate. McCarthy, however, sniffed at the extravagant attention being paid to Kennedy. Reporters, he informed us one day, are like blackbirds perched on a telephone wire. When one flies off, the others always follow.

Then one night during the Nebraska primary campaign, he joined several of us having dinner at the old Blackstone Hotel in Omaha, a restaurant of great charm and mediocre steaks, to chat about the contest. The Nebraska primary that he had touted as the first real test of his confrontation with Kennedy was, he had come to realize, meaningless. In fact, he went on, most of the primaries didn't mean much if anything. If the Democrats were going to defeat Richard M. Nixon in November, McCarthy was the only candidate who could do it, because he was the only candidate who could reach beyond the Democratic base, by which he clearly meant blacks and union workers.

Listening to this new line, we realized that he now was determined to have the Oval Office, not just the satisfaction of ending the war in Vietnam. And he was now doing the predictable politics-as-usual things he had disdained, including disparaging his rivals. The haughty manner that had once seemed a manifestation of his personal reserve now appeared to be simply garden-variety arrogance. He had become just another candidate and not a particularly attractive one.

It was also becoming apparent, although only in small ways, that he didn't feel as connected to the legions of young people who had been so important to his campaign. I noticed that I was hearing something different from Alice Krakauer, a nineteen-year-old sophomore psychology major who taken a leave from New York University to work in the McCarthy pressrooms in each successive primary state. She didn't seem to have as much direct exposure to the candidate as had been the case, and she was a little puzzled by some of the things he appeared to be doing and saying. She was clearly upset when he said in one interview, for example, that he might be able to accept as the party nominee Vice President Hubert H. Humphrey, the one candidate now seen as carrying the banner and Vietnam policy of Lyndon Johnson. You had to wonder how he could hold the loyalty of the Clean for Gene brigades, the kids he now dismissed so airily.

As it turned out, he didn't. He won the Oregon primary. But in doing it, he began taking shots at Kennedy, suggesting that Kennedy had been winning primaries in Indiana and Nebraska because of his great appeal to "the less intelligent and less well-educated voters of the country." Now they were competing in Oregon, he added, a state with "a reputation for passing a most enlightened judgment on candidates." The implication of McCarthy's words angered Kennedy's allies and disheartened some of those who had put their own lives on hold to join what they believed to be a high-minded crusade.

Then, at the tumultuous Democratic convention in Chicago, there was the matter of his performance when what an investigating commission later called a "police riot" erupted. With many of his supporters among the antiwar protesters targeted by the police, McCarthy started to leave town, abandoning those who had worked for him all through the primary season to the mercies of the angry cops, with no powerful leader to protect them. He changed his schedule only after several of the senior figures in his campaign and the Secret Service warned him that if he left, the Chicago police would lock up everyone wearing a McCarthy button. So much for loyalty to your troops.

The image of McCarthy as a liberal martyr who fought the good fight for the right reasons lived on in the minds of enough people in the next generation to encourage him to continue running for president every four years or so. Within the political community, nonetheless, his reputation as a political cynic hardened, particularly when he quit the Senate Foreign Relations Committee immediately after his 1968 campaign failed and then retired from the Senate in 1970. But there were enough people who were never let in on the little secret to enable him to earn good lecture fees and rally a few supporters for those new if ultimately unsuccessful campaigns for the presidency and even for a return to the Senate he had disdained so publicly.

As time passed, McCarthy rewrote the history of his 1968 campaign to make it more interesting or at least self-aggrandizing. In 1978, ten years after his challenge to Johnson, he wrote a magazine article in which he chastised the press for failing to see how well he was doing in New Hampshire until it was all over. It was revisionist history—the press had trumpeted his rising strengths in the last two or three weeks of that primary campaign. So I wrote a column for the *Washington Star* about Gene McCarthy "whining" again. The next morning McCarthy called to tell me I was all wet. He wasn't a whiner. After listening for a while, I began to laugh, and McCarthy demanded to know "what's so damned funny anyway?" To which I replied, "Listen to you, Gene, you're whining right now." To his everlasting credit, he laughed.

A few years later I managed a small retribution for his continuing complaints about the press. I ran into him one day, and he set off on a rant about how ridiculous it was that he was always called "former Senator McCarthy" every time he was mentioned in the news media. Why, he wanted to know, wouldn't it be just as sensible to refer to him as "poet McCarthy" or, citing another item on his résumé, "former first baseman McCarthy"?

I wrote it off as just another example of a McCarthy put-down. But as it happened, a few weeks later I was having lunch with an attractive thirtyish woman in Duke Zeibert's restaurant only to be approached by the table-hopping former senator. It became clear immediately that this young woman, a reporter from a small Midwestern television station who was in Washington on an internship, didn't know who Mc-Carthy was or had been in his glory days. So, as introductions were in order, I introduced him as "former first baseman McCarthy." He rolled his eyes at me and hopped on to the next table.

Barbara Bush is another classic example of the mistaken perception that becomes written in stone. She has been seen by the nation for years as the strong but kindly matriarch of the Bush family and the quintessential first lady with her ubiquitous pearls and grandchildren and little dog Millie. And she has been given well-deserved praise for her efforts to promote literacy.

But those who have dealt with her as staff workers in campaigns and while her husband was in office paint a different picture, of a woman who is harsh with the help, class-conscious—she has been known to refer to others who "came from nothing"—and summarily elitist in her attitudes toward those outside her set and particularly toward any-one with the audacity to run for office against her husband or sons. Those who have had unhappy experiences with "Bar," as she is called, are unwilling to describe them for publication, however, because they fear retribution. "When you're on her shit list, it's a bad place to be," a vice presidential adviser once told me as he explained why I was on the list—because I had been quoted in *The Wall Street Journal* in 1979 saying of her husband that "when you hold him up to the light, he doesn't throw a shadow."

Barbara Bush has been a careful steward of her own image most of the time. The one exception was in the 1984 campaign when she de-scribed her husband's opponent for vice president, Geraldine Ferraro, as a "four-million-dollar—I can't say it but it rhymes with *rich*"—ap-parently referring to the Ferraro-Zaccaro net worth and who knows what else. She later apologized for calling Ferraro a "witch."

Ferraro, the candidate from Queens, apparently was a real bone in the throat for the Bushes of Kennebunkport. The day after the vice presidential debate in that 1984 campaign, George Bush was overheard by a boom microphone telling some longshoremen in New Jersey that "we tried to kick a little ass" in that event, then, spotting the mike, he added: "Whoops, oh, God, he heard me! Turn that thing off." He compounded the political misdemeanor later by explaining to reporters that it was "an old Texas football expression." That one took the prize for lame.

Barbara Bush's image has been helped along by her Republican friends gushing praise time and again. In 2001 a conservative commentator named Barbara Olson, wife of the newly minted Republican solicitor general, Ted Olson, was quoted in a British newspaper on why women had less influence in the Clinton administration than with George W. Bush in the White House.

It was a preposterous notion on its face, but Olson put it this way: "Look at Bill Clinton's mother, as opposed to George W.'s mother. Is your mother a barfly who gets used by men? Or is your mother a strong woman who demands respect for her ideas and always received it?"

Barbara Olson, who later died in the plane that crashed into the Pentagon on September 11, apologized that her "choice of words" had been "very unfortunate." But those words also were part of a pattern of hostile wisecracks about the late Virginia Kelley that were totally off the mark. I knew Clinton's mother a little from going to the racetrack with her on two occasions. Yes, she took a drink from time to time, and yes, she loved playing the horses, which she did with relish and the smarts of a veteran handicapper. But she was an unaffected and charming woman who had worked hard to raise a son to become president of the United States after losing one husband to an accident and another to alcohol before marrying Richard Kelley late in life. She didn't grow up in Rye as the daughter of a magazine publisher and go to Ashley Hall and Smith College before marrying the son of a United States senator. She didn't deserve being put down.

None of this suggests, of course, that the press was criminally delinquent in failing to depict Barbara Bush more accurately. She was not an elected official who had been chosen by the country to perform a public duty. She may not have been a terrible person, but neither was she Mother Teresa.

No one would argue, either, that the susceptibility of the press to false images and political propaganda is, in itself, a mortal threat to the republic. But newspapers and perhaps the television networks have a responsibility to be more accurate in the way they depict public figures, even if it requires some nuance from time to time. The best newspapers sometimes provide such coverage, but they don't do so enough to compensate for the dumbing-down of the world carried out by television networks and local stations and, of course, the cable channels programmed for the mindless.

One of the victims, for example, has been George H. W. Bush, husband of the sainted Bar and forty-first president of the United States. I thought Bush was an empty suit interested in the presidency far more for a line on his résumé than for what he might accomplish in improving our society. But the image of Bush as "the Wimp" was a bum rap that he never put behind him. It stuck to him when *Newsweek* magazine published a cover story in 1987 headlined FIGHTING THE "WIMP FACTOR" and when George Will, who was known to lunch occasionally with Nancy Reagan, called him a "lapdog" for President Reagan while he was vice president. Bush tried to overcome the perception. You don't call someone a wimp when he has been the youngest Navy pilot shot down in the South Pacific at nineteen and has played first base for Yale. But most of his efforts were characteristically inept. The most grotesque was his claim in an interview with CBS News that he had shown he wasn't a wimp by suffering through the death of a three-year-old daughter from leukemia. You could prove he was a jerk and a preppy and a toady to Reagan, but not a wimp. He was, after all, the only former president so far who had made a parachute jump after leaving office. Would a wimp do that?

For a time, Tip O'Neill seemed to be a victim of stereotyping as the old Irish pol from the streets of Boston (although it was actually Cambridge) who reached his lofty station as a wheeler-dealer. His girth, red face, and big nose made him ideal for the part. In fact, however,

O'Neill was the quintessentially issue-oriented liberal who rose to prominence in the House of Representatives as a man regularly ahead of the curve on issues. He was one of the very first in the House to question Lyndon Johnson's course in Vietnam. And he was the liberal leader on a whole series of programs for the disadvantaged.

In the late 1970s and early 1980s the Republicans raised a lot of money deriding Tip O'Neill. And polls showed the stereotype was widely accepted as he became more and more the butt of the late-night comedians and conservative commentators. He helped the process along by shying away from television until his friends and advisers pressed him into more frequent appearances. In the end prolonged exposure turned the verdict of the polls around to the point that after he left office O'Neill suddenly showed up starring in an American Express commercial.

Sometimes the images of political leaders are a product of their interests and associations. The fact that the images are dead wrong is beside the point.

Running for the Democratic presidential nomination in 1984, for example, Senator Alan Cranston of California was considered by the press and by the liberals who rallied behind him to be an expert on national-security and weapons issues because of his prominent role in demanding a nuclear-weapons freeze. We learned how hollow that reputation was during a ninety-minute debate limited to arms-control issues that was held in Des Moines early in the campaign. Although he had the most supporters packed into the Civic Center auditorium that day, it was clear that all three of his rivals sharing the stage—Walter Mondale, John Glenn, and Gary Hart—were vastly more informed on the issues.

A generation earlier, in the late 1950s, I had a similar experience in learning what was behind the image of Governor W. Averell Harriman of New York, who had earned a reputation as a diplomat for expertise in foreign relations and particularly the Soviet Union. Harriman had little or no interest in the governorship or the concerns of the people of New York he was supposed to be serving. He was a remarkably unpleasant man who treated his staff badly and looked down his patrician nose at most of his constituents. He was the heir to a Union Pacific Railroad fortune who had spent much of his youth playing polo and lustily pursuing the young things who spoke through their almost clenched teeth. His adherence to the Democratic Party, many suspected, was far more a matter of political convenience than a matter of conviction.

He saw his exile to Albany after his election to the governorship in 1954 as largely a vehicle for another stab at the Democratic presidential nomination in 1960, riding on that foreign-policy credential. The problem, however, was that his reputation seemed to be based on sand. His renown for being "the first" to recognize the threat embodied in Joseph Stalin, State Department insiders reported, was a case of adopting the analyses of bright foreign-service professionals who worked under him as United States ambassador to Moscow. And the views he used to deliver to any audience who would listen were largely boilerplate right out of *The New York Times*.

In any case, his design for the future was stymied when another wealthy New Yorker, Nelson Rockefeller, defeated him for reelection in 1958. The press had subscribed almost uncritically to the notion of Harriman's expertise; the voters were less easily charmed or perhaps just not interested.

Most often the distorted images are a product of, to use a favored phrase of poll takers, a "defining moment" that is given a lot of attention in the press and especially on television. Thus, President Gerald R. Ford was by no means a clown but was easy to caricature as Bozo after he bumped his head on a helicopter door and winged a golf spectator by shanking a drive off the first tee. So when he stumbled over the issue of the Soviet role in Poland in his 1976 debate with Jimmy Carter, it was easy to chalk it up as "another" Gerry Ford bumble.

Similarly, Carter was characterized as sort of prissy from the moment he came into the White House. He had that soft southern speech and gentle public persona, and he presented himself as a sharp contrast to that hard guy Richard M. Nixon. Soon, however, the perception grew that he was "soft" because he didn't use the muscular language many presidents favor. And the image was reinforced by such things as his brief collapse while running a 10-K race and his report on an aggressive rabbit that he had had to fend off with a paddle while he was fishing in a Georgia pond one day in 1979. The "killer rabbit" story was particularly damaging because it became further "evidence" of his putative weakness after the Iranians seized the American hostages in Tehran three months later and Carter's personal qualities became a critical issue in the 1980 campaign he lost to Ronald Reagan.

But the notion of Carter as "weak" was ludicrous to those who knew him. If anything, he was often too unbending and always massively self-assured. His failure as a political leader was his refusal to play the image game he disdained once he reached the White House. He never understood that "playing politics" often translated into "showing leadership."

We reporters generally love stereotypes because they make our jobs easier. It is less trouble to categorize someone as a liberal or conservative than it is to explain the nuances of his political persona and ideas. And the Carters were easy to stereotype as borderline rednecks. The president's sister was a Bible thumper who rode around on a motorcycle, and his brother, Billy, ran a gas station and drank beer all day before he foolishly strayed off to Libya and signed on as a lobbyist for Muammar Qaddafi.

But the caricature of Billy Carter missed some interesting facets of his life. He was, for example, remarkably well-read. He subscribed to a variety of newspapers across the country, and he was a regular patron of the public library in Sumter County, leaving every week or so with an armful of books. One of Jimmy Carter's most praiseworthy traits, in my view, was his refusal to apologize for or put down, even privately, the relatives who sometimes embarrassed him. Indeed, on one occasion he urged me to "get to know Billy better; you'll like him."

In our quest to label everyone we seem to be particularly hard on losers. Barry Goldwater was not a frightening nut, and George McGovern was not a fool. But both lost presidential elections by staggering margins and were exiled for years by their own parties.

We didn't even get the story of Richard Nixon straight. Feeling some guilt for being hard on him in 1960, deservedly or not, most of us fell for the notion of the "new" Nixon when he finally captured the White House in 1968. We tried to approach his stewardship with open minds. It turned out, as the Watergate tapes disclosed in such stark language, we were right the first time.

12

THE GOOD—OR AT LEAST
DIFFERENT—OLD DAYS

A few days after the capture of Saddam Hussein, Madeleine Albright, the former secretary of State, went to the Fox News Channel bureau in Washington to be interviewed—probably a bad idea. While she was being made up, she speculated with the man in the next chair, Morton Kondracke, about the possibility that the White House had hidden away Osama bin Laden to be produced—voilà!—shortly before the presidential election in November. It was the particular item of political gallows humor many Democrats were repeating in those days—the dreaded "October surprise" to end all surprises!

To Albright's chagrin, Kondracke, a commentator for FNC as well as a veteran newspaper and magazine reporter, quickly quoted her on the air without asking if she meant her comment to be on the record. In the brief flap that followed, she protested that she had been joking and Kondracke replied she had not been smiling. But the idea of a secretary of State from the previous administration publicly making such a snide crack is hard to accept. She said it and got burned by a reporter she had known for years. Kondracke, despite his insistence that she hadn't been smiling, was distressed enough to send her a dozen roses as a peace offering.

This episode probably would not have happened in the political journalism of twenty or thirty years ago. I am not going to play the role of old fart arguing that everything was better in the old days. The reporters and editors in the generation that followed mine were as capable as we were. Their stories were usually insightful, thoroughly reported, and well written. But I would argue with some vehemence that political reporting was very different twenty or thirty years ago. It was possible for a public official or politician to have a social conversation with a reporter without the fear of being victimized by a journalistic cheap shot.

And I am going to argue that the ethic that applied in those days served our readers and viewers—the potential voters—better than they are served today. It permitted us to get to know the politicians far better than is usually the case now. In turn, those insights improved our coverage, and in many ways not always obvious.

The fundamental problem today is simply the numbers of those who fancy themselves covering politics because they ride a candidate's press bus in Iowa or New Hampshire or, in the case of television in particular, because they interview the candidates. Most of their reporting is derivative because they don't have their own sources. If they didn't have *The Des Moines Register,* they would be hard-pressed to cover the Iowa caucuses. Without *The Boston Globe,* ditto for the New Hampshire primary. Without *The New York Times* and *The Washington Post,* these reporters would be lost in the general election campaign.

So much of the current political coverage focuses on the spectacle of the campaigns—a spectacle often caused by the presence of the press mob—rather than the dynamics of the relationship between politicians and voters. Too often those "covering" a campaign are being led by the nose by the candidates' advisers and spokesmen. If they didn't have the daily candidate schedules, they wouldn't know where to go every morning.

The campaign coverage itself is too often focused solely on what is visible to the naked eye and to the cameras, which is just dandy with the campaign managers who control that raw material. You want to see my candidate telling you all about how he will protect the environment, come right over here to the edge of this beautiful lake. You're wondering who has blue-collar support, we'll show you the candidate surrounded by guys in their union jackets. You want someone who loves the old codgers, we've got nursing homes up the wazoo. The pictures are worth thousands of words, easily trumping those long analyses of their positions on complex issues like acid rain or pension-plan scandals or Medicare.

There are too many outlets and too many people scrambling for a crumb of news to report breathlessly. A generation ago the political-reporting corps, except at national conventions and during the last month of the general election campaign, was made up of correspondents from about a dozen major newspapers, three television networks, three newsmagazines, and two wire services. These were the reporters who covered off-year elections and such obscure events as the Western Governors' Conference and, by doing so, built a huge cadre of sources and an equally deep fund of knowledge about issues and demographics.

Now we have CNN and FNC and MSNBC and CNBC. We have Internet magazines—Slate and Salon, most notably—that apparently reach a large audience of nerdy young readers with too much time on their hands that they might spend better shooting eight-ball. We have countless niche magazines whose writers suddenly pop into a campaign to find out where the candidates stand on religious persecution or rye bread with caraway seeds. We have cute reporters from MTV asking "the tough questions the regulars don't dare ask." And we have those darling youngsters from Children's Express doing those candidate interviews. Aren't they precious?

Nor should we forget the foreign press—the correspondents and television crews from all over the Americas, Europe, and the Far East who show up at every major campaign event. I took part in a briefing on the 2000 New Hampshire primary arranged by the State Department, and more than fifty of them showed up. They are, through no fault of their own, the most derivative of all because (1) they have no sources on the ground or knowledge of how things work, and (2) the candidates and their advisers usually ignore them. If you are running for president of the USA, who cares what they think in Oslo or Paris or Bogotá? You can worry about that later. Maybe, like George W. Bush, you can continue to blow them off after you arrive at the White House.

Just the size and diversity of the media changes the nature of the coverage. There are too many reporters willing to do whatever it takes to get a story no one else has written. So many of them rush to their computers or microphones with what I like to call "technical exclusives"—meaning stories no one else prints or broadcasts because no one else gives a damn about them. The "story" about Madeleine Albright's wisecrack falls into that category. Who cares?

What we should care about, however, is the epidemic fear among politicians these days that a reporter is going to "get" them. The only way to avoid that happening, many of them clearly believe, is to avoid reporters assiduously. They're just out to nail me with a bad quote, so to hell with them! For many of those running for high office, the notion of trusting a reporter is simply laughable. What's in it for me?

It was not always that way. For most of the last forty years I was one of no more than ten or fifteen reporters who covered campaigns all over the country for the Senate and House or governorships and even a few mayoral elections. I concentrated on two kinds of campaigns. The first were those with some potential for national interest down the road—meaning those in the largest and most competitive states and those involving candidates who might reasonably become possibilities for national office. The second were those that were intrinsically interesting enough or important enough to make a good story and, I would confess to myself if not to my editors, might be fun to cover. Forget Utah and Indiana.

I spent a lot of time in Arkansas in the 1970s. I first went down there in 1974 because I had heard that an icon in Washington, Senator J. William Fulbright, was being given a stiff challenge in a Democratic primary by some unknown hayseed governor named, would you believe it, Dale Bumpers. As it turned out, Fulbright was not just being challenged, he was being beaten. And, as it turned out, Dale Bumpers proved to be the best hand-to-hand campaigner I ever saw.

Four years later I was in Arkansas again, covering another Senate race and, more to the point, discovering what baseball scouts once called "a young phenom" named Bill Clinton, running for governor in 1978 and already being seen by the home folks as a ripe presidential possibility for 1992. I agreed with those forecasts enough that I returned to the state every year or two and kept up with his administration. I kept track of such things as his reform of the education system in the state. What I didn't take seriously enough were all the stories in Little Rock about "the governor and the ladies," as one local politician put it. If those stories were true, I figured, the newspapers in the state would have found out and nailed him. Bad figuring on my part.

Many of those I thought had great promise never fulfilled it.

I first got to know Mario Cuomo when he was running for mayor of New York in 1975. He lost to Ed Koch, but he was intriguing because he was so thoughtful, so articulate, and so argumentative. I remember being impressed when a young reporter from a student newspaper at Columbia University asked him a few questions about the problems with New York's ambulance service that showed her to be knowledgeable about the issue. When the press conference was over, Cuomo put his campaign schedule on hold and spent almost an hour talking to her about the most arcane aspects of the ambulance issue.

I followed Cuomo throughout his career as New York's secretary of state, lieutenant governor, and finally governor. At each stage he was a politician steeped in the substance of the issues on his plate and intellectually engrossed in most of them. It made for interesting conversations if not always good stories. Along the way, I realized that the force of Cuomo's personality made him one of those politicians who can persuade their constituents to forgive them on issues on which they disagree—in his case, the death penalty being the most obvious. And as a campaigner, the Cuomo I knew was one of those of whom the professionals like to say, "He fills the screen." He showed that to the country with his speech at the Democratic convention in 1984, a speech that immediately put him on everyone's list of leading prospects. But he never wanted it badly enough to bring himself to run.

I enjoyed Kevin White, the mayor of Boston, for many of the same reasons. He was perceptive and funny, and like all mayors, he had to deal repeatedly with difficult and vexing issues on which he could never win politically. The most traumatic was the turmoil in his city that grew out of the court-ordered racial integration of the public schools. In a city that prides itself on being seen as "the Athens of America," the violent and implacable racism seemed foreign and, to White and others, embarrassing. I would stop in Boston to see him every few months. We would have lunch or I would ride around the city with him during campaigns. He was a charmer and a bit of a rogue but always good company. Sometimes we would have an early-evening drink on the third floor of the city-owned mansion on Beacon Hill, looking out over the Public Garden. I would listen to him boast about his world-class city and rant about how he had once again screwed up his relationship with *The Boston Globe*.

I imagined the nation might be captivated by a similar exposure to Kevin White. But his only chance for a place on the national ticket passed when George McGovern chose Tom Eagleton instead in 1972. He thought about running for the Senate against a vulnerable Republican, Edward W. Brooke, in 1978, but the prospect of life in the Senate didn't appeal to him. He asked me once what a senator did all day, and when I started describing the committee hearings, conference committees, markups of legislation, and the like, his eyes glazed over. He was too accustomed to making decisions, and he realized that senators' answer to most problems is to hold a public hearing because they lack the power to do anything real.

I went to Alabama to see George Wallace regularly because he was a continuing force in national politics during three presidential campaign cycles from 1968 through 1976. And there were other aspects of the state's politics I found intriguing about which I could write pieces that people interested in politics could expect from a good newspaper. I was particularly interested in the 1986 campaign for governor because I believed that if Bill Baxley, a liberal who had made a strong record as attorney general, could be elected, he could move the Democratic Party in Alabama away from the Wallace taint and into a role in the national party. That was a tricky business for the states in the Cotton South, with their white voters turning away from what they perceived as a "black party." As it turned out, Baxley's personal relationship with an attractive reporter in Montgomery came to light during the campaign and stopped him cold. But he was a smart and interesting companion for dinner or a couple of pops.

What I found particularly fruitful was the time spent with potential presidential candidates long before they were well enough recognized as such to become fodder for television. Tom Ottenad of the *St. Louis Post-Dispatch* and I were the only two reporters, for example, who traveled with Jimmy Carter when he made his first national trip in January 1975 as someone admittedly testing the waters for a 1976 campaign. In that same period I spent weekends on the road with two Republicans considered potential challengers to President Gerald R. Ford, former Attorney General Elliot Richardson, and former Treasury Secretary John B. Connally. In each of these cases, I produced a story for my newspaper, then the *Washington Star,* and came to know the politicians a little better, sometimes a lot better.

Not all the candidates I covered were able to deliver on the winter-book odds. Until he lost a campaign for reelection in 1974, for example, I thought Governor John Gilligan of Ohio was a strong possibility for the Democratic ticket in 1976. He was smart, substantial, and personable, although sometimes acerbic. But he was doomed politically when, already under fire for raising taxes, he was asked at the state fair if he would attend the sheep-shearing contest and replied: "I don't shear sheep, I shear taxpayers." Bad answer. I had a similar notion of the future about Republican Richard Thornburgh when he was governor of Pennsylvania from 1978 through 1986. I made yearly trips to Harrisburg to spend an evening over hamburgers and Scotch with him. When he tried to move his career to the Senate after a few years as attorney general, the voters of Pennsylvania turned him down.

The rules that governed relationships between reporters and politicians were always somewhat ambiguous and remain so today. "Off the record" used to mean that you couldn't use the material at all. Now it seems to mean essentially the same thing as "not for attribution," which means that you can use the material and characterize the source but not identify him or her by name. Then there are "background" and "deep background," conditions under which you are supposed to use the material only in ways that it cannot be traced. You cannot, for example, characterize a source as "close to" or as "someone attuned to the thinking of" the politician involved.

For many years I was part of a group of a dozen political reporters who held occasional "deep background" dinners with politicians, many of them obvious presidential aspirants, to get to know them better and to understand their intentions. The original group was formed in 1969 as Political Writers for a Democratic Society (a takeoff on the antiwar protest group Students for a Democratic Society). The successor in the 1980s and 1990s had a slightly different cast and was called the Healy PAC after, for some reason lost in the mists, Bob Healy, the longtime political writer for *The Boston Globe.*

We operated under what was once called the Lindley rule, named after a long-ago columnist for *Newsweek,* Ernest K. Lindley. This dictated that anything you used from one of the dinners had to be used without any attribution at all. You were not free even to refer to the conversations having taken place. If you wanted to write that George McGovern had a dandy new plan to win the Democratic nomination, which he described to us in my living room one night in 1970, you had to do so on your own authority, with no attribution. None of us tried it, because we knew such a story with no source would not go down well with editors. So we all missed a chance to be ahead of the curve, even if not for the first time.

But the dinners were often learning experiences, one way or another. When Hillary Clinton came to dinner at Al Hunt's house in Cleveland Park to talk about her health-care plan in 1993, we asked her about Lani Guinier, a woman President Clinton had chosen to head the Civil Rights Division of the Justice Department. It was a choice of considerable political importance to the liberal community and, of course, black Americans. Guinier was a personal friend of the

Clintons'—they had attended her wedding—as well as a highly respected academic. But some of her writing about race issues set off the yahoos on the far right and was arcane enough so it had to be read thoughtfully to be understood. The capital was boiling with speculation about whether Clinton would go through with the nomination. But when we asked Hillary about her old friend Lani, she acted as if she hardly knew the woman, so we inferred that Guinier was going to be thrown over the side. As indeed she was a few days later. But the more important lesson we learned that night was that with the Clintons, loyalty can be a one-way street. Judging by the way he jerked around his cabinet and friends in the Monica Lewinsky affair, Bill Clinton confirmed the suspicion that he expected to receive it but didn't feel obliged to repay it.

When it came to ground rules, the best device I ever encountered was one employed by the late Harry J. O'Donnell, a onetime Associated Press reporter and then longtime political flack in New York for people as diverse as Thomas Dewey, Nelson Rockefeller, and John V. Lindsay. When Harry told you something that he intended to be truly off the record, he would preface it by saying, "This is not for use." You didn't have to figure out how to contrive the attribution so readers couldn't figure it out, on the off chance that the reader cared.

O'Donnell also followed practices that made him extremely valuable to both his principals and the reporters covering them. If I came upon some information that might be damaging to, for example, John Lindsay, I would take it to O'Donnell. Sometimes he would simply say, "That's interesting," which I would take to mean it was true but that he could not confirm it even off the record. Or he would say, "You're going to be sorry if you write that one," which meant it was false. The critical point was that he never lied, and reporters knew it. And the candidates and officeholders for whom he worked were spared many stories that were both mistaken and damaging.

Editors don't like stories with unnamed sources, but that is because they are editors locked up in their offices rather than reporters trying to find out what the hell is going on, often something that can be determined only by promising a source anonymity. Editors love to insist on the "two-source rule," meaning you have to have at least two people confirming whatever you report or you have to have the writing skill to get around the rule. As a practical matter, the good editors are the ones who hire and promote reporters who do not have any axes to grind and do have the judgment to know which sources can be trusted. That's what political writing is all about: judgment and detachment.

The rules rarely were mentioned in most of the one-on-one conversations I had with politicians over the years. And if they were ambiguous, there was also a tacit understanding that I was trying to get to know them and learn more about their thinking and not to write a cheap-shot story if, for instance, one of them were to remark on the physical attributes of the cocktail waitress. If any of them had ever confessed a felony, I might have rushed to the telephone and yelled, "Get me rewrite and stop the presses."

But that didn't happen very often. Instead, I learned other things. That Ed Muskie could fly into towering rages. That Jimmy Carter was a lot more sophisticated and worldly than he sometimes seemed. That George Wallace was a remarkably insecure man and an extremely lonely one. That Richard Nixon had a prurient interest in other people's sex lives but tried to keep it hidden. That Hubert Humphrey's eyes would tear up with emotion when he described things he had done for Minnesota. That John Connally was a great wit and storyteller. That the stoic Michael Dukakis could show intense emotion when his family was involved. (He also spoke Greek and Spanish with some emotional flair, leading members of his 1988 campaign staff to joke that Dukakis could really connect with an audience "in any language but English.") That Ronald Reagan could be painfully naïve. (He was shocked at a television docudrama about Dwight D. Eisenhower's World War II love affair with his driver, Kay Summersby.) That both Bill Clinton and Bob Dole could have temper tantrums aimed at some lowly staff person.

Even if the candidates were more accessible, there are fewer reporters who seem to enjoy spending time with politicians. Some of those on the beat are candid in their dislike for both the people of politics and the playing field on which they compete. You gain the impression that many of the newcomers to political writing are there simply to get their tickets punched before they move up life's ladder to become an editor or bureau chief, both jobs that are far less rewarding or fun than covering the elections.

The downside of spending time with politicians is, of course, the risk of becoming too close to people you cover. There continues to be a debate in the newspaper business about the danger that political reporters will become so friendly with a candidate or candidate's advisers that they will be unable to summon the personal detachment essential to covering the beat. It is a legitimate concern. We all have had candidates we grew to like and enjoy, as I did Morris Udall in 1976, for example.

And we count many political professionals as friends with whom we enjoy lunch or dinner or a couple of jars or a ball game or a day at the track. I've confessed in the past to going into the tank for Robert Strauss, a man of intelligence, political acuity, and great wit who is, among others, good company.

The relationship between the consultants and reporters has become increasingly important as the consultants have assumed greater roles in more campaigns and the reporters have become more dependent on them to learn how the wind is blowing in a particular contest. We both know for whom they are working, so we don't expect them to sell out a candidate. But we both know, as well, that we are going to be dealing with each other down the road every two years or perhaps more often as another round of elections approaches. So trust on both sides is important. They are in a position to give us "guidance" from time to time, but they won't do so if we violate their trust. By the same token, the political professional who lies to me unnecessarily never gets another chance to do it again. It is always possible for the campaign operatives to simply say that they can't talk about something we want to talk about. So lying is rarely justified. And people involved in politics—whether candidates, campaign strategists, or reporters—tend to have very long memories.

Some of the professionals I have known for decades, and they have become personal friends. I have known and trusted John Deardourff, a Republican consultant, since the early 1960s, and I have counted another Republican, Jim Lake, as a friend since 1976, the same year I came to know Jody Powell, press secretary to Carter, and Peter Hart, a Democratic poll taker of keen insight. Ray Strother, a Democratic media consultant, has been a friend and sometime companion at the track for twenty years. Some of the best have died untimely deaths—Bob Squier, Bill Hamilton, and Paul Tully, among them.

Tully was a Democrat who usually could be found working for the most liberal candidate in the field. He had an encyclopedic knowledge of the political demographics, much of it obtained from the computers of Mark Gersh at the Committee for an Effective Congress. Tully was more than numbers, however, because he was remarkably perceptive about how a campaign ploy or a whole campaign might play out. He was also a man of impressive appetites for meat and drink with whom it was always both instructive and pleasant to spend an evening.

Tully was one of a small handful of political operatives who were valuable to candidates because of their ability to size up situations instantly and forecast the consequences. Like computers, they can tell the candidate instantly that if he does this thing he is planning to do, the voters will respond this way, his opponents that way, and the press still another way. They can also figure out immediately which groups of his supporters may be encouraged or offended by the initiative.

Fred Dutton, a Democratic lawyer in Washington since the Kennedy administration, played that role in several campaigns beginning in the 1960s. So did such Republican counterparts as John P. Sears, also a Washington lawyer who came along with the first Nixon campaign in 1968, and Stuart Spencer, a Californian who has been one of the two or three wise men of the Republican Party for forty years.

Nor are all the smart guys in Washington. There are political reporters, party leaders, professional consultants, and full-time activists all over the country whom I have known for twenty or thirty years, in a few cases even longer. I have relied on them to know what was hap-

pening in their bailiwicks and to tell me what they can. These are people for whom politics is a calling or a consuming interest who don't
deserve to be denigrated, as they often are, as hired guns or campaign
junkies.

In Boston there is a streetwise political operator behind every tree.
It was no surprise to anyone in the trade, for example, when the John
Kerry campaign sent Michael Whouley to Iowa to save his bacon in
the precinct caucuses. If the problem had been elsewhere, it might just
as easily have been Chuck Campion or Charlie Baker, his partners in
the Dewey Square Group. Or any of a dozen other Boston professionals who show up in campaigns all over the country every four years.

The point is that these are sources of information to whom I have
gone back year after year. I suspect that many of those covering campaigns now don't know a lot of these people or their successors. These
are reporters who show up with a rental car and a road map in even-
numbered years or even only every four years. It's not their fault. Their
employers, looking at the declining voter turnout and often declining
ratings, don't think politics is worth enough attention to assign reporters to the story four years around.

Whatever their sources or lack of sources, political reporters now
are very different. More of them, including two or three of the best,
are women. Most of them follow a lifestyle quite different from the
questionable example set by me and many of my colleagues. Where we
were partial to martinis and Scotch, steaks and ribs, they prefer wine
and broiled fish or salads. Where we whiled away the hours playing
poker or gin rummy, they are more likely to go to the hotel fitness center for a workout. They tend to have dinner with one another; we usually sought out some political operative or candidate from whom we
might learn something. They tend to go to bed before closing time.

We used to have a good time covering presidential campaigns. We
could write songs poking fun at candidates without worrying about
how it would look or sound in print or on television the next day.
Riding the whistle-stop train of candidate Robert Kennedy during the
Indiana primary campaign of 1968, we did a takeoff on "The Wabash

Cannonball," playing to his reputation for being ruthless. It began this way:

> *Oh listen to the speeches that baffle, beef, and bore*
> *As he waffles through the woodlands and slides along the shore.*
> *He's the politician who's touched by one and all,*
> *He's the demon driver of the Ruthless Cannonball.*

> *He came down to Logansport one sunny April day,*
> *As he pulled on through the depot you could hear the Hoosiers say,*
> *He's the heir apparent, full of chutzpah, full of gall,*
> *I'll bet he wants our helping hand on the Ruthless Cannonball.*

Subsequent stanzas dealt with his rivals—McCarthy and Indiana Governor Roger Branigin, a politician known to take a drink who was running as a stand-in candidate for Lyndon Johnson.

> *There goes Roger Branigin, the Hoosiers' favorite son,*
> *He doesn't want the office, he only wants to run,*
> *His highballing days are over, he's riding for a fall,*
> *They're noted for long memories on the Ruthless Cannonball.*

> *Now good clean Gene McCarthy came down the other track,*
> *A thousand Radcliffe dropouts all massed for the attack,*
> *But Bobby's bought the right-of-way from here back to St. Paul,*
> *'Cause money is no object on the Ruthless Cannonball.*

Our critics will say we were frivolous people, but the authors of that one included David Broder and David Halberstam, to whom that label hardly applied even in 1968.

We were also given to playing on our own highly individual weaknesses, the kind that become known to everyone after a few years on the same beat. One target was one of the most energetic reporters in the group, R. W. Apple, Jr., of *The New York Times*, known universally as Johnny. Apple was the only true gourmet in the political press corps.

He knew all about food and wine and later in his career proved as much with encyclopedic reports on his indulgences all over the globe. Johnny was also rather proud of his reputation for a sensitive palate, which made him an obvious target.

A couple of days before the 1976 Republican convention in Kansas City four of us arrived at a local restaurant of some renown, the Savoy, without reservations. We were about to ask the maître d' if he could squeeze us in when the sharp-eyed Walter Mears of the Associated Press spotted Apple's name on the reservations list. It was about nine o'clock, and Apple was down for a party of four at that very time. So Mears blithely announced, "Apple, we booked for nine P.M.," and we were promptly shown to a table in a rear room.

A few minutes later Apple arrived with a colleague from the *Times,* B. D. Ayres, and was obviously in high dudgeon at the theft of his reservation. But there were now tables available, and Johnny and Ayres were shown to one across the room. Apple saw us all watching him and snickering and shook his head. The message was clear: Some guys have no class. We decided to make amends by sending a bottle of wine to Mr. Apple, please, a clay bottle of Lancer's rosé that retailed for about a buck twenty-nine. Now Apple was really incensed. He wasn't about to drink a carbonated rosé. What if someone saw him? But his companion was quite willing to drink it, so Apple was mortified until he came up with the solution of keeping the bottle under the table.

We did serious work, but we were not always serious people.

There are also stark differences in career paths from generation to generation. Political reporters in my set did not labor and scheme to become editors of their newspapers. We thought we had the best job imaginable, so why would we want to get stuck in an office listening to reporters whining about what the copy desk did to their stories?

What may be the biggest difference, however, is the focus on television. In my generation only a few newspapermen found long-running places in television, usually by some happy accident. But once we tried it, we learned that television changes your life in some positive ways. It makes it easy to get a table, even a "good" table, in Washington restaurants without claiming to be Johnny Apple. More to the point, it brings the lecture fees that allow you to live like an editor without having to be one. It provides, in effect, a subsidy to compensate for the reality that editors and publishers rarely deliver on their big talk about how the backbone of the newspaper is the reporter. They know they can get away with paying us in bottle caps because we love the work.

It has become increasingly difficult for me to maintain the same level of interest in politics at the highest levels in the last few years. The campaigns have become too stylized and programmed to score that magic hit on network television. And the candidates are less interesting and too clearly packaged. It has become easier to understand why so many Americans eligible to vote don't take the trouble to do so.

13

FOOLED AGAIN, AND AGAIN

*T*here have been times, of course, when voters seemed to be paying enough attention and, as a result, sent a message so clear that both the press and politicians understood it. The Democratic gains in the midterm congressional elections of 1974 and in the election of Jimmy Carter in 1976 are cases in point. Both were in large measure a response to Watergate. Americans were sick of what they were seeing in Washington and blamed the Republicans.

But never in my forty-plus years covering national politics has the electorate behaved as purposefully as it did in 1992 and 1994. The turnout in that 1992 presidential campaign was up sharply, 55.2 percent of those eligible compared with 50.1 in 1988 and, more to the point, a reversal of the trend of the previous two generations. And the message from those who voted was direct. Americans wanted change, and if you can imagine, they believed it could be accomplished through the ballot box. You could call it a triumph of hope over experience, or perhaps a suspension of disbelief.

The first indications that 1992 might be something special came in the contest for the Democratic presidential nomination. Approaching the election year, the conventional wisdom in both the political community and press, in Washington and elsewhere, held that President George H. W. Bush was essentially unassailable. Early in 1991 he had directed a war in the Persian Gulf against Iraq that seemed an immaculate operation—great pictures of bombs falling on target, minimal American casualties, total victory. And this president was a nice man who cooked hamburgers for his grandchildren. What a guy. Bush's approval ratings in the polls were off the charts, as high as 85 to 90 percent in some surveys.

So the Democrats who might have been expected to challenge him—Richard Gephardt, Al Gore, George Mitchell, Bill Bradley, Sam Nunn, Lloyd Bentsen, Jay Rockefeller, and, once again, Mario Cuomo—began to run for cover. They all had some excuse for their political timidity, but the conventional wisdom, which is usually correct, applied to most of them. They didn't want to risk their careers attempting to defeat an incumbent they saw as undefeatable. None understood that picking your spots—waiting for "the right time"—is a luxury not available in national politics.

The only leading party figure who was not intimidated by the prospect of challenging an incumbent who had won a war was Ronald H. Brown, the personable chairman of the Democratic National Committee. He had overcome imposing political obstacles of his own in becoming the first black American to win the chairmanship, so he knew something about beating long odds. With Paul Tully supplying the figures on demographics and describing the kind of coordinated campaign that had been used successfully by Democrats in state elections, Brown argued that Bush was vulnerable and that the party's major contributors should be prepared to support a serious run at him, Persian Gulf War or not.

By late 1991, however, the field was not impressive to the naked eye—six candidates who at first blush looked like a fresh version of the "seven dwarfs" that had competed for the Democratic nomination in 1988. This time the group included a sometimes difficult African American serving his first term as governor of Virginia (Douglas Wilder); two liberal senators of undetermined potential and largely unknown nationally (Tom Harkin of Iowa and Bob Kerrey of Nebraska); a retread close to qualifying as a hardy perennial (Jerry Brown of California, otherwise still known as Governor Moonbeam); a former one-term senator who had been fighting cancer (Paul Tsongas of Massachusetts); and a governor of, would you believe, Arkansas (Bill Clinton).

In fact, this denigration of the two fields was never legitimate. The field in 1988 had included several substantial people with impressive records and sound experience who did not deserve the ridicule they got, most of it from critics far less accomplished. The same was true four years later. Although Wilder and Brown might be dismissed as fringe candidates with essentially no chance to be nominated, there were still four politicians of some quality seeking the 1992 nomination. Harkin was the favorite of several liberal unions, and Kerrey appealed to other liberals who liked his often quirky style. As governor before he moved to the Senate, Kerrey was romantically involved with Debra Winger, which is not all bad politically.

But it was easy for the wise guys on television, the pundits on the op-ed pages, and indeed, many newspapers to write them off as trivial and hopeless. And as for Bush, once someone assumes the office of president of the United States, many of us in the press and too many other Americans accord him great stature. We don't feel free to recognize how ordinary—or, in the case of George H. W. Bush, how shallow—he can be.

As it turned out, however, 1992 proved to be a very different year, one in which the voters said, in effect: We are so frightened about our economic future that we are going to try using the ballot as a weapon to change things.

The first signals came from the response to Paul Tsongas in the New Hampshire primary campaign. The self-anointed experts doing little or no reporting on the ground passed off Tsongas's show of strength in polls as just a product of his history as a former senator from a neighboring state. It obviously wasn't his personal appeal to the voters; Tsongas, as he ruefully conceded to his friends, had all the charisma of a cauliflower. So it had to be the hometown connection. It wasn't. The notion that many Americans know the senator from a neighboring state is laughable; most of them don't even know their own. In any case, Tsongas had not run a statewide race for thirteen years when he began his presidential campaign.

As the campaign evolved, it became obvious that Tsongas had reached the Democratic-primary voters with his message. He had published an eighty-six-page booklet entitled "A Call to Economic Arms" in which he outlined his ideas for restoring America's manufacturing base. To people in a state that had lost its five major banks to mergers and fifty thousand jobs in the previous four years, a state in which bankruptcies and welfare rolls were at record levels, he was talking about a relevant question indeed.

Thus, on a cold Sunday afternoon nine days before the primary, he showed up at a meeting in a cafeteria at Daniel Webster College in Nashua and found perhaps five hundred people there, people not bused in by the well-oiled Tsongas Machine, which didn't exist, but people who arrived two or three at a time because they wanted to hear what he had to offer. Tsongas spoke for forty minutes, then for almost two hours took questions from his listeners, many of whom cited particulars from his booklet. No more than a dozen or so left the hall before the candidate ran out of steam. Reporters who had shown up just going through the motions of doing our jobs and prepared to scoff, myself included, were impressed bordering on bowled over.

That special interest in Tsongas was not enough to sustain his campaign to the end. Although he won the primary, Bill Clinton finished second and pronounced himself "the comeback kid" for the network cameras because he had not been buried by his unconvincing denials about Gennifer Flowers and his dissembling about his draft dodging and marijuana use—which did not, thank heavens, include inhaling.

In a sense the Tsongas approach had even helped bail out Clinton by allowing him, an inveterate policy wonk as well as inveterate womanizer, to focus the late stages of the primary campaign more on the issues of governance and less on the "bimbo eruptions" that unsettled his staff. As the comeback kid starring on every home screen and as a forceful and articulate advocate, he was now the clear favorite for the nomination.

The contrast was sharpest between the serious purpose of Paul Tsongas and the George Bush campaign in the Republican primary, in which Bush was fighting off a challenge from conservative commentator Patrick J. Buchanan. Rather than confronting the economic concerns of New Hampshire voters, the Bush operatives heralded the president's eleventh-hour trip to the state with newspaper advertisements urging Granite State voters to come to the airport to "see *Air Force One.*" And Bush himself gave the voters what he called a "special treat" when he introduced Arnold Schwarzenegger at a campaign rally—to applause that, incidentally, dwarfed that for the president himself.

Even after Buchanan polled a respectable 37 percent of the vote to Bush's 53, the president's campaign managers and most of the press and political community continued to view the president as unassailable. He won that war in the Persian Gulf. How could they forget that so soon?

A second indicator that the 1992 campaign was different came in March when Ross Perot appeared on the Larry King show on CNN, where he later took up almost permanent residence. He allowed that if voters in all fifty states put him on their ballots, he would run for president. His aggressive attacks on, for example, the way the federal government was dealing with its fiscal and debt problems touched a nerve with many Americans. And there are always some voters convinced that what this country needs is "a good businessman in the White House, somebody who's met a payroll." So it was no surprise when the next morning lines of petitioners showed up in state capitols all across the country seeking to put Perot on their state ballots.

Again, television was driving the story. We now had a colorful independent promising to "look under the hood" and find out what was wrong—how could you beat that? The voters of 1992 were serious enough about seeking solutions that Perot was soon running second to Bush in the national surveys.

Neither Tsongas nor Perot was able to capitalize on his instant and obvious rapport with a large segment of the electorate—voters who, reporters found, were taking their responsibility to help choose a president very seriously indeed. Nonetheless, both built enough continuing support to reinforce the perception that this was a different election.

Tsongas had neither the stamina nor the money to compete with Clinton the rest of the way. Nor was he imposing enough as a personality to be seen as the leader of a national ticket. The Arkansas governor, by contrast, was showing himself to be a masterful campaigner who understood that the people were demanding change and were looking for someone who they were convinced would deliver. Nonetheless, there was still a significant minority of Democrats who remained committed to the candidate from Massachusetts even after he had withdrawn. Clinton's nomination may have appeared inevitable and inexorable by late winter, but in the New York primary in April Tsongas won 29 percent to Clinton's 41 and Brown's 26. Some 280,000 Democrats supported the thinking man's candidate, almost one third of the turnout, causing some momentary ambivalence on his part about the possibility that he might return to the campaign.

After his initial explosion into the national consciousness, Perot began to self-destruct by showing repeatedly that there were legitimate questions about whether he had the temperament for the White House. The fact that he quit the campaign entirely in July and then returned in August was only one of several indicators that Ross Perot was marching to some other drummer.

Still another sign of 1992 as a very different year was the popular interest in the debates during the general election campaign. Although the usual pattern is a declining audience as candidates confront one another a second and third time, the reverse was true this time around. The audience grew over the three debates to roughly 100 million in the final showdown between the three candidates. These voters of 1992 were serious about making a choice and what they hoped would be a change for the better in their economic prospects.

The ultimate proof, of course, was the final result. An incumbent Republican president, George H. W. Bush, captured only 38 percent of the vote. This was an avuncular figure, a "nice man" with a long résumé who had won this dandy war to save our access to oil for future generations. But he lost 62 percent of the vote to two candidates carrying enough political baggage to sink the *Lusitania*. Clinton won with 43 percent despite the accumulating evidence that he was a trimmer. Perot took 19 percent despite, among other things, his penchant for hiring private investigators to look into conspiracies that never existed. It was an amazing showing for a candidate who dropped out of the campaign in July because he claimed the Bush campaign was planning to sabotage his daughter's wedding.

The voters had spoken and their demand was obvious. Although the Republicans were grousing that 43 percent was "no mandate" for Clinton—a complaint that, by the way, they never made when Richard Nixon won with 43 percent in 1968—there was no denying that the new president had been handed a mandate for change.

So what happened? Approaching the congressional elections of 1994, nothing much had changed in Washington. In the eyes of many Americans, the politicians were still doing things the same old way. There was gridlock and partisan excess on Capitol Hill and few results on the most significant issues.

Taking office, Clinton had declared the need for health care the single most pressing crisis facing the American people. Thirty-five million Americans lacked health insurance, and something had to be done about that before he tackled the fundamental problems with the tax system, the entitlement programs, and the national economy. The priority for the health-care issue was evident in his decision to assign it to a task force led by Hillary Rodham Clinton. Such a portfolio had never been given to a first lady, not even Eleanor Roosevelt, but this was a new and different breed of first lady, a competent lawyer steeped in many public concerns.

When the time arrived for the 1994 congressional elections, however, neither the health-care problem nor any other major concern had been resolved. Perhaps surprisingly, the Americans who had trusted the system to bring change in 1992 decided to try it one more time in 1994. Their frustration and anger crystallized into a reaction against the president that overlooked some strides he already had made toward a healthier fiscal situation. More to the point at that moment, it crystallized into a decision to throw out the bums in Congress who had failed to change their ways—meaning in this case the Democrats who had controlled both the Senate and House of Representatives for so many years.

The gulf between the insiders of press and politics in Washington and the rest of the country was never more evident. A series of stories I was reporting for my newspaper, the Baltimore *Sun,* showed me just how wide the gulf had become.

Early in the year I had chosen three congressional districts with different political contexts to visit once a month as a way of measuring the extent of the change in Congress likely to take place in November. One district was the Fifth in North Carolina, where a Democrat had retired and trends seemed to favor a Republican takeover. Another was a marginal or "swing" district in the suburbs of Philadelphia usually decided by a point or two. And the third was the Twenty-eighth, centered on Rochester in upstate New York, in which a strong incumbent Democrat, Louise Slaughter, was facing a more serious challenge than in any previous campaign.

The theory was that if the Republicans won all three seats, a landslide was in the making or, conversely, if the Democrats held two of the three, they probably would hold their losses to a minimum. As it turned out, the Republicans won two of the three—Louise Slaughter was too popular—but won a landslide anyway.

The most revealing element of the exercise was the way the controversy in Washington over a health-care bill was viewed by voters in, for example, Winston-Salem compared with how it was seen in the capital. By late summer, health care was being handled or mishandled not only by the White House but also by several different committees on the Hill. The hope seemed to be that a bill could be put together from these various centers of power, much like ordering from Column A and Column B on a Chinese restaurant menu.

To those of us who lived within the Beltway, this all seemed possible enough, even routine. After all, there were good people in both parties in both houses of Congress who were both expert on the health-care issue and serious legislators—Democrats like Pat Moynihan in the Senate and Dick Gephardt in the House, Republicans like John Chafee in the Senate and Nancy Johnson in the House. It would all work out in the end.

But in Winston-Salem what people saw on their television screens every night was a kind of legislative chaos. Committees would meet in closed sessions, and senators or congressmen would emerge with some cryptic comment about how things were progressing or not progressing. The voters in Winston-Salem thought it was a terrible way to make law, and in September they were telling me it was time for Congress to shut down the process and try to make a fresh start the next year.

Eventually that sentiment permeated the collective consciousness in Congress and they gave up. What they did not do, however, was return to the problem the following year—or ever. After the Republicans won both houses of Congress for the first time in forty years, Clinton seemed to forget about the high priority he had assigned to health insurance. He was so spooked by the Republican ascendancy that we soon found him musing aloud—at a press conference in Jakarta— about how he might be able to find a way to support, of all things, a prayer amendment. He apparently hadn't noticed that Jews voted four to one for Democrats in the elections.

The Republicans' sweep in 1994 was not just a case of the voters rising up spontaneously to use the process for change. Some of their success clearly could be traced to the "contract with America" that their clever leader, Newt Gingrich, came up with as the theme for their campaign. But it was plain to those of us who covered the campaign that the result was less a testament to the Republicans than a reaction against the isolation and insulation of Washington politicians, who were mostly Democrats. Some very able people—Speaker of the House Tom Foley comes to mind—were defeated that fall.

The nation now had experienced two consecutive elections in which the voters demanded change in terms that could not be denied. So what happened?

Again, almost nothing. The Republicans, particularly in the House, interpreted their success in the election as an endorsement of their agenda on social and cultural issues rather than a demand that Congress deal with national problems. Rather than focusing on education, they concentrated on trying to undermine abortion rights. Rather than dealing with health care, they tried to repeal the ban on assault weapons that had overwhelming popular support. There was a great deal of talk about the need for moral leadership even before Bill Clinton's dalliance with Monica Lewinsky had begun.

The Republicans did have one prime political accomplishment, with the craven acquiescence of the Democratic president. Throwing aside sixty-five years of Democratic Party principle shortly before the 1996 election, Clinton agreed to a welfare-reform bill that fell far short of what he had proposed in his 1992 promise to "end welfare as we know it." The requirements for job training, day care, transportation, and the like were forgotten.

By the time the 1996 campaign rolled around, many voters apparently had realized that their hopes for affecting change with their political leverage were not going to be fulfilled. President Clinton defeated Bob Dole, longtime Republican leader in the Senate, in an election that attracted the lowest voter turnout since 1924. That might qualify as the nadir of nadirs, at least until Al Gore and George W. Bush competed four years later in what proved to be the equivalent of a scoreless tie.

The 1996 election sent one little frisson of hope through the body politic. With Clinton assured of his second term and no longer needing to please all the people all the time, he might have seemed free to do the things that are most difficult politically—most important, an overhaul of the Social Security and Medicare programs that would ensure their viability for several more generations. Instead, the high points of the second term were his waffling over "that woman, Miss Lewinsky" and the ultimate partisan brawl over his impeachment.

So much for making democracy work and all that stuff.

14

WHY I'M FED UP

Books like this one are supposed to end with an optimistic chapter describing "solutions" to the problems the author has been whining about in all the previous chapters. But I doubt there is any easy way—or, for that matter, any way at all—to fix the things that are wrong with American politics today. They are too deeply rooted. They are too much a part of a pattern of mindless behavior in our culture. We worship all the wrong gods—money, celebrity, and television, most notably. We listen to the loudest voices. We pay obeisance to false standards imposed on us by those with an axe to grind. We are too lazy intellectually to go beyond the glib language of politics.

After fifty years as a newspaper reporter, most of them covering national politics, I am both fed up and dismayed. American politics has gone sour. We have made a series of mistakes in choosing our presidents. And the blame should fall on the press as well as on the politicians who sometimes behave badly and on the citizens who don't pay attention and too often don't bother to vote.

It is not something I am comfortable admitting. I have loved newspaper work and have never considered doing anything else. It has paid me far less than I could have earned elsewhere. It was worth it because of the people—other reporters and editors—with whom I was able to spend my career. I have never lost the thrill of covering a "good story"—meaning something either significant enough or intrinsically interesting or both, which is the definition of the Big Story. Nor has seeing my own byline in the paper stopped giving me pleasure. Any reporter who claims he doesn't read his own stories is either lying or trying to rationalize his way into becoming a well-paid flack for an airplane manufacturer.

I have enjoyed immensely getting to know the country as well as I have. For all our faults, Americans are decent people and marvelously complex. As a young reporter sometimes covering cops, as the police beat was known, I learned how venal people can be at their worst. But they are the exceptions. Most Americans want to do the right thing and make the future more promising for their families and their neighbors. They are ambivalent about politicians. They either look up to them, which I consider a mistake but understandable, or they view them with mindless contempt and hostility, which is also a mistake.

But these days most Americans are unwilling to make any effort to, as horsemen like to say, improve the breed. They pay little attention to politics, and surveys show they find that campaigns have little relevance to their lives. As a result, the news media fail to pay enough attention either, or at least not enough to project an accurate picture of politics and its role in our lives. Such a picture could be compelling enough to draw more people to the polling places.

The result of the sickness in our system has been three presidents in a row who were embarrassments or disappointments or both. George Herbert Walker Bush was the classic empty suit. He was, by the testimony of his friends and many who worked for him, a nice man but not one who belonged in the White House. He wanted the office and the title as a vindication of his public career but not as an opportunity to improve the lives of his fellow citizens. He disdained "the vision thing," meaning any grand plan for the future. His son George W. Bush has been an embarrassment who has combined ignorance and arrogance, saved only by shrewd political advisers and his own cunning.

If he has any understanding of what this country stands for, it wasn't apparent in the petulant decision to attack Iraq without direct provocation or in his cavalier disregard of the constitutional rights of our citizens. His cocky dismissal of our allies abroad is something we will be living down for years.

By contrast with the Bushes, Clinton did have goals for our society he wanted to accomplish. And he was well grounded on and captivated by substantive issues, a true policy wonk. But he was so self-absorbed—he cried out for approval in all things—that he missed his opportunity to take the steps he knew were needed. Because he was so much smarter than either of the Bushes, Clinton's failures were especially stinging for those who expected better.

I agreed with Ronald Reagan on few if any issues. I thought his economic and fiscal policies were disastrous, and the invasion of Grenada a national shame. But it was always clear that he had values he wanted to defend and goals he wanted to achieve. You might not agree with them, but you could not question the sincerity with which Reagan pursued them. To some degree, the same could be said of all the other presidents who served during my time in Washington—John F. Kennedy, Lyndon B. Johnson, Richard M. Nixon, Gerald R. Ford, and Jimmy Carter. They all had failings, but they were all serious people. The same cannot be said of George W. Bush.

So how did we get this way?

One easy answer is money. Despite the reforms on campaign financing enacted after Watergate in 1974 and the limits on unregulated "soft money" contributions imposed largely because of John McCain, it is still worthwhile for those with large amounts of money to buy into the process. Oil companies on the one hand and Big Labor on the other prove that in every campaign. The result is that a George W. Bush can raise money by the tens of millions of dollars to overwhelm those who rely on the meager public funding provided by the 1974 law.

Money matters, however, only to the degree that voters are gullible and allow themselves to be swayed by the television commercials, targeted mailings, and door-to-door canvasses it finances. If voters were more discriminating, those TV spots might not have the influence on public opinion that can now be detected in every campaign. The political media consultants are paid top dollar because they know just which approaches will work with which group of voters. But their techniques might be less effective if the press covered the campaign with somewhat more sophistication and skill in focusing the voters' attention on serious concerns.

Even allowing for the failures of the news media, there may be ways to lessen the influence of the commercials. I have always thought they might be less valuable a weapon if commercials were required to carry an identifying message—PAID FOR BY THE GEORGE BUSH CAMPAIGN— in large type across the screen for the full thirty or sixty seconds they are on the air. The most damaging negative commercials, those that attack an opponent on questionable grounds, might be used less frequently if campaigns were required by law to provide copies of their TV ads to their opponents a full twenty-four hours before they were scheduled to be shown, thus permitting rebuttals that might level the field.

Neither of those ideas is likely to come to anything, however. The politicians in Congress don't want to put a burden on their own campaigns. Many of those who voted for the McCain-Feingold legislation did so only because they became convinced it was politically too risky not to do so. It is no secret that John McCain is not the most popular member of Congress with his colleagues.

The power of big money is not the only insidious influence on our politics today. Another is religion and particularly the religious right, the intensely conservative Protestant fundamentalists who have become such a controlling force in the Republican Party and a factor that no one in either party can safely ignore. These are the people who say that if you disagree with them, you are taking a morally unacceptable position because God is on their side. In their moral certitude they are strikingly similar to the Islamic fundamentalists who are so controlling in the Middle East. Our experience in Afghanistan alone should be a warning to those in this country who seem to believe the principle of separation of church and state is just a nuisance that interferes with their plans.

(In the interests of full disclosure, I must note that although I was brought up as a Protestant, I have been an atheist my entire adult life. I do not proselytize, however. Nor do I question the faith of others. I just don't want to be obliged to accept someone else's faith as a factor in my government. If John Ashcroft wants to hold a prayer meeting and advertise his piety, let him find someplace besides the Justice Department to do so.)

The rise of religious fundamentalism has been a compelling force in the hardening of partisan lines and the decline of civility in our political life. It is far more difficult for legislators to negotiate compromises on issues if one side is accusing the other of taking an immoral position, which is too often the case in Congress today.

For reasons I've never fully understood, the fundamentalists are overwhelmingly Republican. A 2003 Pew Center survey that found support for George W. Bush and for a generic Democratic candidate dead even at 42 percent each also found Bush leading by 26 percent among respondents who go to church at least once a week. Poll takers say the gulf is even wider among those who count themselves as born-again Christians, as does Bush himself.

The single most divisive issue is clearly abortion rights. The fundamentalists support a constitutional amendment that would forbid abortions even when the life of the mother may be in danger. If you disagree, many of them will call you an evil person or perhaps even a murderer. This is one where there is no compromise.

Although overwhelmingly in favor of abortion rights, even Democrats tiptoe around most religious issues because they are aware that so many Americans claim to be committed to religion. It is a rare and brave politician—the late Senator Ernest Gruening of Alaska, a rare man in many ways, was the only one in my time—whose official biography does not list a religious affiliation. Those who identify themselves as Unitarians are often suspected of being closet agnostics or atheists. And those Democrats who want everyone to love them are sometimes tempted to yield on the church-state question—as Clinton did so ignobly on the fundamentalist demand for prayer in the schools after the Republicans won Congress in 1994.

The failure of our politics is a product of something more basic, however, than the influence of money or religion. It begins with mistaken ideas about the standards we should use in measuring politicians, up to and including the president of the United States.

The answer does not lie simply in identifying with one political party or the other. There are, to be sure, significant differences between Republicans and Democrats. Some of them are simply demographics. Republicans are proportionately more white, more Protestant, more middle-class, more affluent, better educated, and more often found running either small businesses or giant pharmaceutical and oil companies. Republicans wear more flags in their lapels, but most of the kids doing the fighting probably come from Democratic families. I noticed that George W. Bush's daughters didn't volunteer to fight in Iraq.

The truly significant differences lie in their attitudes toward government. Democrats are more inclined to rely on government action to solve national problems and perhaps restore some economic and social equity. Republicans are more interested in cutting taxes and government regulation they view as intrusive. Both parties talk a lot about patriotism and national defense, but the Democrats don't often suggest a lack of spine on the other side.

Both parties have changed over the last two generations. The Democrats have become more centrist on social questions, perhaps because there is no issue of overriding importance comparable to the demand for equal rights for black Americans, perhaps because they are yielding to the conservative pressures within their own ranks. Democrats can now favor the death penalty without being drummed out of the tent. Democrats now put almost as much stress as Republicans on reducing street crime.

Republicans who earn a political dividend from kowtowing to the fundamentalists also pay a price. Those who hold moderate views on social questions are barred from the party's national ticket, as was Governor Tom Ridge of Pennsylvania in 2000 because of his support for abortion rights. Moderate Republicans are, in fact, a vanishing breed in Congress and not likely to be replenished. When former Governor Tom Kean of New Jersey was the strongest Republican possibility to succeed Christine Todd Whitman in the Senate, he decided against it because, as he put it, "I wouldn't fit in this Senate."

Whitman's own experience is a classic example of the power of the religious right. She had burst onto the national stage by winning the governorship in New Jersey and seemed to have a boundless future. But she supported abortion rights and was not considered "reliable" by the born-again Christians. So George W. Bush could not even give her anything better than administrator of the Environmental Protection Agency, where her own views were far more protective of the environment than those of the White House. After a decent interval, she returned to New Jersey.

Identifying favored candidates by party, however, is not an approach that will improve our politics. Although it makes a significant difference which party is in charge—no Democrat would have chosen Ashcroft in the first place, to cite an obvious difference—anyone involved in the political community for a few decades recognizes that there are admirable people on the other side. Saying so may be frowned upon by the most devout partisans these days, but it has not always been that way, particularly in Congress.

I can recall in the early 1990s, for example, two Republican members of the House of Representatives making a point of telling me that Barney Frank was a hell of a good member and should not be condemned for the mistake he made becoming involved with a homosexual prostitute. Barney works hard and keeps his word, they assured me. I doubt that would happen in a climate in which the House majority leader, Dick Armey, referred to Frank as "Barney Fag" and then giggled about this little sample of whatever passed for humor at the two-bit Texas college where he taught economics. With too many of the extremists, civility is equated with weakness.

Nor does the road to more rewarding politics lie in checklists of issues, even if editorialists, civics teachers, and the League of Women Voters may think this is the proper route to good government. There are sometimes issues so overarching in their importance that they can be used as litmus tests. Civil rights was one of them. And before it was over, so was the war in Vietnam. There have been no issues of comparable reach on the horizon since that time, however, although for many Americans the support for or opposition to abortion rights is an essential position to win their ballot. There are also at least a few for whom protection of the environment is critical.

Most of the questions that occupy center stage in campaigns are less emotionally charged, however, and should be viewed as less important by voters. No one is going to walk through a wall to reduce the capital-gains tax rate or the size of the foreign-aid budget. The debate over most of the things government does is largely over methods, not basic tenets of either party's dogma.

One underlying weakness in our campaigns is that they tend to focus on issues that presidents of the United States cannot control or even influence a great deal—and the press seems powerless to make that point clear to voters. In several campaigns of the last forty years, Democratic candidates—notably Hubert Humphrey, George McGovern, Jimmy Carter, and Michael Dukakis—have been tarred by the Republicans with being "soft on crime."

Just what this means isn't clear in most cases. Nor is it clear how this would affect the conduct of their presidency. In fact, the federal government and the president have a very limited role in crime prevention or law enforcement. Presumably the argument could be made that a "soft on crime" candidate might be inclined to appoint judges who hand out light sentences or perhaps reduce federal funding for local police departments, thus encouraging more street crime.

However vague, the professionals on both sides believe the perception of "softness" among Democrats has been extremely damaging to them because it implies a weakness not just in dealing with criminals but on national-security questions. If Michael Dukakis, as governor of Massachusetts, would let Willie Horton out of jail on a furlough so he could commit a violent crime in Maryland, how could we expect him to stand up to the Commies? That wouldn't happen if more voters paid more attention to the basis of the political rhetoric they are absorbing from their television screens every night. But the political operatives dreaming up the thirty-second spots are counting on few people paying close attention. The picture of Willie Horton is scary, and that's what matters.

A second qualifying factor in weighing issues is the priority they are given by the candidates. A Republican candidate may take the required party line and oppose abortion rights, for example, although he has no intention of making the issue an important one in his presidency. He may have no intention of requiring opposition to *Roe v. Wade* as a qualification for the federal bench or the Supreme Court, despite just such a provision written into the Republican platform every four years.

Those inclined to use checklists of issues in choosing a president also must understand that it is almost impossible to anticipate the situations that will confront the new president. Nobody foresaw the 1979 hostage crisis in Iran when they elected Jimmy Carter in 1976. No one predicted when they elected Ronald Reagan four years later that the radical policies of Mikhail Gorbachev would effectively end the cold war and lead to the collapse of the Soviet Union. Who foresaw the Iraqi invasion of Kuwait in 1991? Who could have imagined the terrorist attacks of September 11, 2001? Or could have known how George W. Bush could respond with such a display of strong leadership and then use the war on terrorism as a blank check to attack Iraq? Saddam Hussein was never an issue in the 2000 campaign.

Moreover, the promises any candidate makes are inevitably affected by the conditions of his presidency—the money available and the makeup of the Congress, most notably.

In the end, it is far wiser to focus attention on the kind of people who are running rather than which one seems to have the best plan for providing drug coverage to old folks. What has he done? What do people who know him think of him? What kind of people does he have around him? (For simplicity's sake, I use the male pronoun here, but the questions obviously apply equally to female candidates.)

Most to the point: Is he intellectually honest? Is he comfortable with himself? Does he understand the difference between political adversaries and enemies? Does he have some things he wants to accomplish for the national good? Do you share those goals?

We might even hope to find a candidate capable of ignoring opinion polls and leading Americans in a different direction, then persuading them to follow in large enough numbers to win an election. Politics is an imitative business, and such a candidate, if successful, would give rise to more of the same dimension.

But given the way American politics operates today, it is extremely difficult to see how such a candidate could make it through the process to capture a presidential nomination and win an election. How does he compete with someone with $200 million to spend on television messages that are drummed into the minds of potential voters careless about how they judge what they are being told?

The short answer is that he probably can't make it, although he may come close. After eight months of exposure and 114 town-meeting appearances before the voters of New Hampshire in 1999 and 2000, John McCain defeated George W. Bush by eighteen percentage points, a blowout by any measure and a harsh negative verdict on Bush. The lesson we should have learned from that experience was that the more people saw of Bush, the less willing they were to vote for him. But there never was another similar opportunity for McCain to become a familiar figure to voters in another primary. Instead, the campaign was conducted at a breakneck pace—candidates flying from airport to airport, from state to state every week—that put an even greater premium on the television commercials Bush could buy with his obscene amounts of political money.

McCain made some mistakes, of course. His attack on the religious right during the South Carolina primary wasn't judicious, although it was justified. But the basic problem for McCain was that the voters in those later primaries didn't come to know either of the candidates well enough to make a thoughtful judgment. Instead, these voters were ripe for Bush-campaign claims that, for instance, the senator from Arizona had voted against funding for breast-cancer research and neglected the concerns of war veterans. It was preposterous considering McCain's heroism in Vietnam and the fact that his sister suffered from breast cancer. But it worked.

There was even a little frisson of hope in the Democratic-primary contest in 2000 between Vice President Al Gore and former Senator Bill Bradley of New Jersey, the onetime star known as "Dollar Bill" with the New York Knicks in the National Basketball Association. Gore was a consummate stiff, but he was intelligent and well-grounded in questions of public policy. And his voting record satisfied the influential interest groups within the Democratic Party that are so important in primaries. He was a consensus candidate among Democratic leaders much like Bush was among their Republican counterparts. The AFL-CIO fell behind him early, and so did many of the interest groups on which Bradley might have had an equal or better claim, given his voting record.

Bradley's campaign was intriguing because he chose not to talk down to the voters, as both Bush and Gore were doing. Instead, he argued that because the economic health of the country seemed assured, at least for the nonce, it was time to face broader national problems. And one of the areas that he chose was the continuing awkward and unhealthy relationship between the races. This was counterintuitive in the Democratic Party of the day, where talking about race was considered foolhardy as a political matter. Anyone who became identified with the problems of the cities, for example, was considered to be embracing a political tar baby.

Bradley's strategy was, however, an example of the kind of leadership that might elevate our politics to the point at which someone cares who wins. And when one night in Iowa I asked him somewhat skeptically if race wasn't a risky topic, he replied that he could not believe that Democrats would not respond favorably to what he was saying. It was, in his mind, unthinkable. It was probably, at best, a close question.

In any case, Bradley made a strategic mistake and tried, somewhat belatedly, to compete in the Iowa precinct caucuses in which Gore had solid labor backing. The New Jersey Democrat bought the old theory, discredited in Iowa every four years, that he could bring enough new people into the caucuses spontaneously to overcome Gore's organizational advantages. And then in a debate with Gore he failed to respond forcefully to a trumped-up complaint about his voting record. So he lost the caucuses, which threw him onto the defensive in New Hampshire eight days later. Nonetheless, even then he managed to hold Gore to a 49–45 percent margin, which suggested (1) that he had touched a nerve with a substantial core of Democrats, and (2) that there were enough reservations about Gore to make him a less than exciting nominee. So exit Bill Bradley.

Although there was reason to be encouraged by the candidacies of McCain and Bradley in the hope that there might be a market for better candidates, neither made it through the winter. In the end, money and the party establishments asserted their authority and we were left with one candidate who didn't know anything and another who couldn't persuade voters that what he knew mattered.

What the McCain case suggests in unmistakable terms is the potential value of more time for the voters and the press to function. If primaries were spread out over three or four months, as they were before every state became part of the schedule, the voters would be given a longer look at the candidates. And, potentially very important, there would be time for buyer's remorse if one candidate leaped to the front of the pack in the Iowa caucuses and the New Hampshire primary and then was found to have sailed to Bimini on the *Monkey Business.* At the least, a more leisurely pace would allow reporters to treat the story with the kind of depth it should be given, not simply fly from one state capital to another every week.

I don't think for a minute that such a change in the schedule is likely or even remotely possible. The decision makers in every state fear their constituents won't have any influence on the nominating process. And they don't want to face up to the fact that they already don't have much clout.

In the long run, the only hope for better politics lies in the possibility of better people who can command the public's attention and win on the force of their personalities and the qualities of their service. These are the politicians with a sense of proportion and an understanding of the differences between adversaries and enemies. These are the people who are, to use a favored cliché of this age, "comfortable in their own skin." There have been people out there who might have fit that description but didn't make it for one reason or another. In my experience, Howard Baker, Nelson Rockefeller, and Mario Cuomo were obvious possibilities. But Baker and Rockefeller were victims of bad timing, and Cuomo was simply too resistant to the idea, although I thought he could have beaten George Bush in either 1988 or 1992.

What we are lacking is the will and the way to make such alternatives—and there are many others—realistic possibilities. We need to get beyond the stage at which the single most important credential is the ability to raise huge amounts of money, even when it clearly involves taking on political debts that skew the whole process of government once the candidate takes office.

But if campaigns are to be largely exchanges of images on television, the first priority must be paying for it. That's where it all comes together. Money and television control American politics, and the successful candidate is the one who finds a way to play under those rules. The press seems powerless to change that.

However, raising enough money to fund another mindless campaign doesn't, in itself, make American politics more pertinent to the disengaged potential voters. Nor does it ensure a result more satisfactory than has been the case lately. As JS Gray told me fifty years ago, we get about what we deserve. So I guess we deserve George W. Bush.

INDEX

ABOUT THE AUTHOR

JACK W. GERMOND has been a political columnist for the Baltimore *Sun,* Gannett bureau chief in Washington, and a columnist and editor for the late *Washington Star.* He first appeared on *Meet the Press* in 1972 and has been a regular on the *Today* show, CNN, and *The McLaughlin Group.* He now serves as a panelist on *Inside Washington* and writes occasional newspaper pieces. He lives in Charles Town, West Virginia.

ABOUT THE TYPE

This book was set in Bembo, a typeface based on an old-style Roman face that was used for Cardinal Bembo's tract *De Aetna* in 1495. Bembo was cut by Francisco Griffo in the early sixteenth century. The Lanston Monotype Machine Company of Philadelphia brought the well-proportioned letter forms of Bembo to the United States in the 1930s.